PLAYS FOR
THE PUBLIC

PLAYS FOR THE PUBLIC

Richard Foreman

THEATRE COMMUNICATIONS GROUP
NEW YORK
2019

The publication of *Plays for The Public* by Richard Foreman, through TCG's Book Program, is made possible in part by the New York State Council on the Arts with the support of Governor Andrew Cuomo and the New York State Legislature.

TCG books are exclusively distributed to the book trade by Consortium Book Sales and Distribution.

Library of Congress Control Numbers:
2018053720 (print) / 2018058919 (ebook)
ISBN 978-1-55936-555-0 (paperback) / ISBN 978-1-55936-875-9 (ebook)
A catalog record for this book is available from the Library of Congress.

Cover, book design and composition by Lisa Govan
Cover photo by Joseph Moran

First Edition, September 2019

Contents

Foreword

By Oskar Eustis

IN THE FALL OF 1975 I walked into Richard Foreman's Ontological-Hysterical Theater for the first time, to see his play *Rhoda in Potatoland*. I hated it, and proclaimed that loudly to my friends. I said the same thing the second time I saw it, and the third. By the fourth time I was seeking tickets, I was forced to recognize that I didn't know myself as well as I thought. *Rhoda*, whose songs I still sing to myself, had become an extraordinary and crucial esthetic–philosophical lesson for me. Art provokes, resonates and teaches in deep and complex ways, not all of them conscious. "Like" and "dislike" were not very interesting categories, terms which certainly didn't begin to reflect the varieties of esthetic experience.

That was almost forty-five years ago, and in the decades since I have watched, wrestled with, and delighted in Foreman's work. In the last decade I have had the privilege, and the pleasure, of producing his work at The Public Theater.

Our revered founder, Joe Papp, first gave Richard a home at The Public in the 1970s, and over the next fifteen years Richard directed both his own work at The Public and that of others, most famously his production of Brecht's *The Three-penny Opera*, starring Raúl Juliá as Mack the Knife. That astonishing and thrilling production (which my teenage self also saw a dozen times) is one of the highlights of The Public's history, just as Paul Davis's magnificent poster is one of our iconic images.

Although Foreman came from an esthetic background utterly different than Joe's, Joe recognized the unique brilliance of Foreman's work, and took him into The Public with the passionate advocacy for which Joe was famous. Joe's embrace of Foreman was part of his surprising and vitally important investment in New York's downtown experimental theater. That interest gave support to Foreman, but also to Mabou Mines, Lee Breuer, JoAnne Akalaitis and others who permanently broadened the mandate of The Public. Joe's belief in inclusivity was not confined to racial and demographic diversity: esthetic diversity was also key to his sense of The Public, a big tent whose artistic complexity was as rich as America's democracy.

Foreman is the theater's playful philosopher, whose plays are simultaneously explorations of what it means to exist, personal (if coded) psychological revelation and theatrically brilliant explosions of visual and verbal wit. Deeply influenced by traditions that extend from Gertrude Stein to the Surrealists, his plays trace the workings of his own consciousness as they question the reality of the self, the desire for (and fear of) the other, the unease of the conscious animal in a deeply confusing—and often threatening—world.

It has always been hard to imagine Richard's plays separate from his brilliant productions. His reoccurring production elements—the mysterious omniscient voice who instructs and warns both performers and audience, the strings stretched across the stage and auditorium, the crowded, even cluttered theatrical space that reads as a downtown New York Cabinet of Curiosities—add immeasurably to the depth and brilliance of Foreman's work.

But there's a unique and irresistible joy to reading these plays, as well. In one of his early manifestos Foreman extolled the virtue of theatrical moments that weren't memorable, that created such a sense of otherness that the mind couldn't comfortably retain the elusive immediate moment (the experience of the moment which is, in some ways, the prize Foreman is always seeking). But reading these plays, examining them at leisure without the urgent propulsive forward movement of the theater, reveals beauties and resonances uniquely literary. As the Voice says in *Idiot Savant*: "Message to the performers: Do not try to carry this play forward. Let it slowly creep over the stage with no help, with no end in view." That's not easy to do in the time-bound world of the theater; in reading, we can allow a different pace of cognition.

These plays slip on genres and characters like masks— the Lumberjack lovers of *The Gods Are Pounding My Head!*, the Samurai intellectual Warrior of *Idiot Savant*, the melancholy later-afternoon Parisian intellectual of *Old-Fashioned Prostitutes*—but there is nothing representational about any of these people or places. Underneath them all is a witty but serious examination of our relationship to ourselves, to each other, to the world, to God.

"Experts are confused," repeats the Idiot Savant, but we also hear, "I believe this play by the name of *Idiot Savant*— hopes to become wiser than individual characters within its pages." Whether the play becomes wiser or not, we do. And not only wiser: more awake. Frenchy, one of Foreman's bewildered Lumberjacks, imagines the fulfillment of his desire in an image that can stand in for the desire of all of these characters in all of these plays:

"Because the beloved for whom I was waitin' in desperation appeared suddenly—like an invisible somebody stepping into that light that blinds all lumberjacks—with my eyes melting into that same fire that burns all other fires. The best fire of all. The real fire. The real fire."

Richard Foreman is one of the great, unique voices of the American Theater. Profoundly influential, there is nonetheless no one like him. Reading these beautiful, baffling, delightful plays, we catch a glimpse of the real fire.

New York
July 2019

Old-Fashioned Prostitutes:
A True Romance

PRODUCTION HISTORY

Old-Fashioned Prostitutes: A True Romance. Co-produced by the Ontological-Hysteric Theater (Richard Foreman, Founding Artistic Director; Mimi Johnson, Managing Director) and The Public Theater (Oskar Eustis, Artistic Director; Patrick Willingham, Executive Director). Presented at The Public Theater, New York City. April 30–June 2, 2013. Written, directed and designed by Richard Foreman.

SUZIE	Alenka Kraigher
GABRIELLA	Stephanie Hayes
SAMUEL	Rocco Sisto
ALFREDO	David Skeist

A large paneled room with banquette.

GABRIELLA: Número One.

(All enter. Alfredo goes to mirror, shines it.)

VOICE: End of play.
ALFREDO: OK. When looking into a mirror
    What one sees—goddammit.
GABRIELLA: Is this true?
    Why does one feel
    one is falling towards the center
    of the earth?
ALFREDO: Like this. *(Falls)*
GABRIELLA: The entire earth—
    I force myself to say that.

5

SUZIE: No no no and no.

ALFREDO: Oh yes, I now say.

SAMUEL: During my leisurely promenade
      Through the dark streets
      of the city of the dead and the almost
      dead
      It comes to my mind . . .

      But perhaps, ladies and gentlemen,
      it is best never to speak openly about
      such things.

      But it did happen
      That traveling these streets
      in bright sunlight
      An old man with white hair
      Shabbily dressed, trudging slowly
      in the direction opposite to the one
      in which I was traveling
      carrying a large, soiled cardboard box
      holding what personal belongings
      I could not guess
      But—whispered hoarsely under his breath
      "Go to Berkeley, make film."

      I did not respond.
      But I frowned
      And a few seconds later
      turned to watch him proceed, slowly
      down the street.

(Girls giggle.)

Later in the day
Lying on the bed in my hotel room
I wondered—

SUZIE AND GABRIELLA: Ooo . . .

SAMUEL: I wondered should I have approached him
to ask for clarification.
Was he speaking to me
or to himself?
—yet it seemed appropriate to my concerns—
And my possible
Future.

GABRIELLA: Go to Berkeley, my friend,
make film.

SUZIE: Well, why not?

GABRIELLA: Which could have meant, not the city in sun-
drenched California—

SUZIE: But possibly the long-dead Irish philosopher of ideal-
ism, Bishop George Berkeley—

GABRIELLA: Oooo . . .

SUZIE: —himself,
whose view of reality might be poetically reimagined
as a vision of the world in which experience
itself was but a thin film, spread in illusionary fashion
upon human consciousness.

SAMUEL: So that
"Go to Berkeley, make film," could have meant, "Go
deeper into the notion of the world as
a transparent surface only"—
depending upon the impress of a mental apparatus—
snapping the world into apparent being only—
And this, then Walt Whitman-like figure—vision
or reality—or serendipitous coincidence
of the moment—this was the message—

the gift to me on such a sun–drenched afternoon.
But of course I said nothing to him—
Too shy perhaps.

SUZIE AND GABRIELLA *(Singing)*:
Shy shy shy, terribly terribly shy.

SAMUEL: Avoiding my destiny perhaps.
SUZIE AND GABRIELLA: Shy shy shy.

SAMUEL: Yet another time, another place
Visiting the city of attractive women
—Feeling my soul as if—activated
And through similar fear, perhaps
failing to return the gaze of old-fashioned
prostitutes—smiling at me
extending many gentle invitations.
Here is the person I have been searching for, perhaps.
Her name is Suzie.
SUZIE: Suzie.
SAMUEL: And I
—Make no appropriate gesture in return.
SUZIE: In fact, you enjoy such failure, Samuel.
SAMUEL: Yes—true.
GABRIELLA: Go to Berkeley, my friend, make film.
SUZIE: Samuel expects nothing more than this.
SAMUEL: Nothing more happens. This is true.
SUZIE: You are here, I believe—for the entire afternoon.
SAMUEL: The entire afternoon.

(Alfredo falls.)

To watch
beautiful coquettes, sip tea, or lick at cool mixed

drinks of gin and vermouth, suffering
quietly like the rest of us—
SUZIE: From what do we suffer, please?
From what?
SAMUEL: Who will tell me this?
SUZIE: From what?
VOICE: Samuel remembers images from the past.
An old man carrying a cardboard box. And one,
two, even three—beautiful women—
When unexpectedly—
An image from a film, projected in his presence
sometime within the past ten years, but then again
Who can be certain concerning time, and place?

This film perhaps—of light and moving shadow—
drenched in reality or something
deeper still.
Vista of foreign cities—
Budapest or St. Petersburg, or Shanghai—
old New York, or Vienna, or London?
Who remembers?

—Only one . . . blazing image
inside a restaurant or cafe.
The view through a large window
with individual panes of glass
framed in thin strips of wood
with electrified streetcars rolling by
and a few passersby drenched in that same light.
SUZIE: Is it morning, Samuel, or is it the blinding
afternoon sun—
Which does Samuel prefer?

SAMUEL: —Strange question—which to prefer.
When what I know—perfectly well
is that beautiful coquettes

—trying to attract—or
To distract, rather—my focused attention—

While I, Samuel
No longer young and beautiful, perhaps . . .
SUZIE: —which must be
The very thing we are all trying to reimagine
right now.

(Pause.)

SAMUEL: Double difficulty—this "life" thing
—entering this—difficult "word" thing—
SUZIE: It must all be true.
SAMUEL: Choose a second word—
you DARE NOT choose.

(Pause.)

SUZIE: I think not.
SAMUEL: Inside—and outside
both at once.
SUZIE: Correct as always, Samuel.
SAMUEL: Always correct, sad coquette.
GABRIELLA AND SUZIE *(Leg up)*: Whee!
SUZIE: The outside which is outside—
SAMUEL: Dare I now say—Old-fashioned prostitutes— *(Girls giggle)* which is now effectively spoken.
SUZIE: Oh yes. This reimagined, spoken twice.
SAMUEL: I shall continue to believe this.

SUZIE: I shall continue to agree, of course.

SAMUEL: —Now named *(Holds his head)*—soft, soft season of
  August.

SUZIE: I would rather testify to hard, this hard August.

SUZIE AND ALFREDO: January
  February
  March
  April.

SAMUEL *(Pause, thinks)*: OK. Following this long, brutal summer
  There does exist
  This—

SUZIE: Oh my goodness.

SAMUEL: —Hard August.
  Where daily cocktail hours shuffle
  through agitated boulevards
  as white napkins still crease themselves
  While beautiful prostitutes
  sip afternoon alcohol
  under the roar of distant traffic
  echoing faraway cities
  in a drift towards the light, dappled, swirling . . .

SUZIE *(Thinks)*: May I come carrying my own glass, to sit close
  beside you?

SAMUEL: Yes. Please do that.

  (Pause, they drink.)

GABRIELLA: Her name is Suzie.

SUZIE: Suuuzie . . .

GABRIELLA: And she is very beautiful—
  Though a bit sad sometimes
  And my name is Gabriella, and I
  am a friend of Suzie's.
  I really am.

11

SAMUEL: As you can already tell perhaps, words
I've been saying, are words that tumble back and forth
in my head.

SUZIE: I understood those words to come from
secret thoughts.

SAMUEL: It must be true.

SUZIE: I had the feeling they came
from a secret part of the body, obviously.

SAMUEL: In one sense—this is true.

SUZIE: Oh, I'm never wrong
When every word you've said
—has been spoken by accident.

SAMUEL: Yes—but does anyone really believe me?

SUZIE: All such things are things I believe—
And yes, I did say—a simple coquette—
I did say—Old-fashioned prostitute.

(Pause.)

Did I say such a thing? Maybe.

SAMUEL: I've said—

SUZIE: Maybe.

SAMUEL: —Almost nothing.

SUZIE: Then who am I? What do I listen to when I speak?

(Pause.)

Yes, my name. My name is Suzie.

GABRIELLA: Suzie.

SAMUEL: Suzie. Yes.

SUZIE: And I too—am now waiting
—at another time
—in another place.

GABRIELLA: A very hard, hard August.

(Alfredo dressed as Michelin Man enters with gun.
BANG.)

VOICE: OK.
SUZIE: I thought I saw a gentleman
    who acted really nice
    but when I took a second look . . . Oh my goodness
    Again
    No
    Bad choice.

(BANG.)

SAMUEL: Arriving finally
    at the city of the attractive women
    I find my soul has been activated
    — But—how to keep this energy
    from dissipating immediately?
SUZIE: I will in no way
    gratify your expectations, Samuel.
ALFREDO: Believe this, friend Samuel—
    Here is the woman
    you have been looking for.
SAMUEL: Do what you can for me, my friend.
    Never allow beautiful Suzie
    to disappoint me.
SUZIE: Never, never never disappoint me.
SUZIE AND GABRIELLA: Wheee!
SUZIE: Is it a possible Samuel we depend upon?
SAMUEL: A mistake
    which profits no one.
SUZIE: Like we depend on no one else in the
    entire world?

SAMUEL: In my careful passage through
  the city of the living and the dead
  —familiar to me, yes—but—no
  longer holding the beauty and excitement
  of many strange cities less well known to me—
  until I discover in turn—right here—
  a method by which I invest this familiar city
  with small moments of the excitement
  for which I still hunger
  —through exhausting use of an imagination
  —able to convince myself
  that around the next corner—

(Alfredo drops barbells.)

GABRIELLA: Oooo . . .
SUZIE: Oh my goodness.
SAMUEL: —Hides—an as yet unknown area of this city—
  Holding yet to be discovered promise
  of unanticipated pleasure and amusement
  Though this effort
  of imagination exhausts me,
  so this familiar city
  sinking back
  into that banal condition . . .
  Spiritually dead.

(Alfredo and Samuel hug.)

GABRIELLA: Oooo . . .
SAMUEL: I do—beg of you, friend Alfredo
  (He grabs Alfredo's lapels)
  —Convince beautiful Suzie.
ALFREDO: Yes. I am Alfredo, your one friend.

14

GABRIELLA: And I am Gabriella. Suzie's one friend.
SUZIE: Suzie.
>   This once only—
>   Listen to me, Suzie.
GABRIELLA: —Grow to be manlike,
>   little friend Alfredo.
ALFREDO: . . . Pressure is
>   building inside me right now.
SUZIE: Yes, me Suzie.
>   Holding onto myself
>   as my body starts shaking inside itself
>   —invisible to everyone but myself
>   while I imagine the following:
>
>   I begin walking down the sun-drenched boulevard
>   in my new polka-dot dress
>   With the skirt that flairs out
>   the way I hoped it would
>
>   while holding a small leather pocket book
>   clutched to the side of my body with frozen fingers—
>   Even though I am smiling a faint smile
>   For what reason really? No reason in fact.

SAMUEL: But in the crowd occupying the many outdoor cafe
>   tables—along that wide boulevard
>   you catch the eye of an appealing gentleman—
>   and you think to yourself, as you come to a stop—
SUZIE: Yes. Smiling—With my back to the sun—
>   thinking as I stop—This is the one
>   who will certify—to my actual existence.
SAMUEL: And you stand there, yes—smiling faintly
>   with the sun behind you,
>   making your hair frizz like a golden halo.

SUZIE: And the crowd on the boulevard
      moving past—in all directions at once,
      But I myself—not moving
      with the eyes of that gentleman upon me
      and—very slowly, like honey dripping
      from a spoon—into a cup of frozen tea,
      my physical self-dissolving—

SAMUEL: To disappear of course, like a slow fade
      from existence—in front of his
      fascinated eyes—and his
      totally focused consciousness
      while this actual—disappearance of your
      physical body—

SUZIE: It could happen.
      I know this could happen—

SAMUEL: —It could happen,
      as if it were indeed melting
      into the world of sunlight behind you.

      And then, finally—
      Would you finally?
      Or then—would it be necessary
      to keep telling the story of your life
      inside your own lifetime—
      when you no longer did exist,
      would those stories however exist—

SUZIE: Nobody knows.

SAMUEL: And who would it be then—that was
      existing in fact?

SUZIE: Right. Be very gentle with me, Samuel.

SAMUEL: Real energy:
      elsewhere.

SUZIE: All questions elsewhere, now elsewhere elegant questions.

SAMUEL: And some day
   perhaps, shall I too
   —re-prostitute one very pure self.

(Pause. Suzie rises and goes.)

ALFREDO: OK. One please.
SAMUEL: Elsewhere.
ALFREDO: —As one prostitute hiding amongst so
   many others. Two and three and four. Where is the
   beautiful Suzie?
VOICE: Not yet, not yet, not yet.
   OK.
GABRIELLA: Did I really hear him say—
VOICE: Not yet, not yet, not yet.
   OK.
GABRIELLA: Did I really hear him say—
   Arriving finally
   at the city of the attractive women—
ALFREDO: —Not true. Beautiful coquette.

(Pause.)

GABRIELLA: Did I really hear him say—
   Yet to be discovered . . .
   Promise of unanticipated
   pleasure and amusement
   —exhausting me completely.

(Pause.)

But I am Suzie's one best friend, am I not?

(DRUM.)

GABRIELLA: Invisible to girls like me.
SAMUEL: Inside out, it means that
    the beautiful Suzie
    has left us behind.

    (THUDS.
        Alfredo leans in, holds ears.
        Suzie leans in, holds ears.)

GABRIELLA: Entering Samuel's world
    just a bit—
    Though I do recognize, such
    half-and-half behavior could be
    my own—problematic—

    (THUDS.
        Holds ears.)

GABRIELLA: Wait a minute—wait a minute—
    Something is wrong.

(Staggers. Pause.)

Wrong, nothing at all is wrong.

(Staggers.)

SAMUEL: Nothing is wrong when you say
    As you did say in the past
    —that Samuel invites trouble, because
    I would tend to agree
    This is true. Is this true?
    Because I desire always that there be
    meaning in all wide awake things everywhere.
    — And now this is true. Is this true?

Because when I come upon some small
portion of my external environment
that seems empty of meaning—

Then I force myself to relax—totally
and true meaning shall then

POUR slowly into
that emptiness inside me
—with no effort on my part.
Not until—beautiful coquettes studying my every move
—and questioning my every statement—
None of this does really happen.
Do you blame ME for this fact?
Yes, I am the one to BLAME.

SUZIE: Because
Someone before our very eyes—fills with rage
— Gentle Samuel.

SAMUEL: But why is this true?

ALFREDO: Oh no!

SAMUEL: Not Suzie? Not beautiful, silent Suzie.

ALFREDO: It will not be Suzie.
Who speaks when she chooses.

SAMUEL: It is Suzie alone who I will believe.
Because I do know
that my rage will be
surprisingly unpredictable.

GABRIELLA: Try to name your unpredictable rage,
Samuel.

SAMUEL: I name it—
Incalculable rage—rage against such "things."
That I do sense
—on all sides of me
Yeah

—In all faces
and in movements of bodies and
in wonderful words that pour forth
only from such
little powerful unexpected surprises.

Am I looking into a mirror?
ALFREDO: Don't say that, don't even think that.
SAMUEL: Mirror images also enrage me when appropriate—
GABRIELLA: Name it! Name it! *(Exits)*
VOICE: And you now ask yourself— During your leisurely
        stroll through the streets of the living and
        the streets
        of the dead—whether you can really believe such
        stories. Plus—simultaneously asking yourself
        whether you exist more in such moments
        —when your whole body is shaking—more
        than you exist when your own story gets fully
        told at last.

        Because—remember—if you disappear by fire
        or if you disappear by time slowly
        melting you against sunlight

        Or if you simply disappear inside your own
        sad story—which you tell simply
        to stop the body from shaking—
SAMUEL: Do I know
        as of today
        the very real world to which
        in fact I do belong?
SUZIE: Well. Let me show you—immediately *(Exits)*
SAMUEL: I feel my question
        has been answered
        with a certain elegance.

(Opens door) Hello! *(Closes door)*
But remembering the question
still eludes me.
Hello!

GABRIELLA: Samuel's dirty, dirty shoes need polishing—
This is one clear fact amongst other facts.

ALFREDO: Of course Samuel is always well dressed—Fact fact
fact.

GABRIELLA: Certain shoes
need extra polish.

VOICE: No world
No world.

GABRIELLA: Old-fashioned in many ways
Coquettes who are sufficiently smart and clever
are deeply satisfied
upon seeing pale, washed-out faces
reflected in Samuel's shoes when they are
sufficiently polished
there at the bottom
of his two tough-guy legs.

VOICE: No world
No world.

GABRIELLA: But think about this, please.
Please.

SUZIE: Oh, Samuel himself
Life—life itself producing
all possible and appropriate—

VOICE: End of play.

SAMUEL: Was I thinking to myself? . . .

VOICE: End of play.

SUZIE: Tell us, please.

SAMUEL: Old-fashioned prostitutes in repose
—to offer appropriate answers
to private mental dilemmas

SUZIE: Samuel will again choose
       something to drink, by which I indicate
       very strong alcohol indeed.
SAMUEL: And Samuel thinks, of course
       strong drink preferable—
       to remaining here
       minus—comfortable, not yet—conversation.
SUZIE: I thought this at least could be
       Samuel's choice—

(Pause.)

SAMUEL: Do we discover
       a mutual subject perhaps?
SUZIE: A strong drink helps, does it not?
SAMUEL: Does it help?

(Pause.)

       Would we talk about
       the quality of such—fine alcohol?
ALFREDO: Ow. Dammit, dammit.
SUZIE: OK. Could the conversation then drift
       towards other things, perhaps?
SAMUEL: You never did ask
       the desirable combination—
ALFREDO: Ow.
VOICE: Imagine no world.
SUZIE: What does the aroma smell like, from way over there?
SAMUEL: It smells like alcohol.
SUZIE: Ah yes, alcohol indeed *(Whirls at rear)* What fun. What
    fun. Oooo. *(Poses against the rear wall)*
       Now tell me, of course—does Samuel earn lots of
         money?

GABRIELLA: My goodness— Nobody in this room has
    as much money as they would like to have.
SAMUEL: I would rather not speak of that.
    I would like to give every one of you money.
    Lots and lots and lots and lots—
SUZIE: Myself—I do prostitution.
SAMUEL: Yes, but . . . I do very little in fact.
    I think I would like to travel.

(Pause.)

SUZIE: Oooo. That's not a good way to earn money, I'm afraid.
SAMUEL: It could be. If I were to scribble stories about
    travel adventures . . .
SUZIE: You probably mean travel guides?
SAMUEL: Oh, yes. Guides
    A kind of guide.

    But I'm afraid my kind of guide
    would be a rather peculiar kind.
SUZIE: How would it be peculiar?
SAMUEL: Well, I already have sufficient money in my pocket.
SUZIE: Yes, I have money too. Why is that?
SAMUEL: Your profession pays very well—
SUZIE: No Samuel, you misunderstand, as usual.

(Pause.)

    My profession is to teach.
SAMUEL: What do you teach?
SUZIE: Private classes.
SAMUEL: Yes, but what? What classes?
SUZIE: —Possibly hard to explain . . .
SAMUEL: Are you successful with TEACHING?

23

SUZIE: Oh quite . . .

(Pause.)

> But thank you for asking.
> Perhaps you should visit my library of old-fashioned
> BOOKS.

(Gabriella blindfolded.)

> Which might help you to understand
> what I do teach.
> The library is very close—it's upstairs in fact.
> Are you not interested—in visiting my books?

ALFREDO: Yes. Goddammit. Help me.

SAMUEL: Strangely enough . . .

ALFREDO: Help! Please.

SAMUEL: It seems difficult for me to move.

SUZIE: Why is that?

SAMUEL: I don't know. My foot doesn't know.

SUZIE: I think I know why.

> It's something I added
> to your drink, Samuel.

SAMUEL: What the hell happens to me now?

SUZIE: I'm not sure, am I?

SAMUEL: I am worried about this.

SUZIE: Don't be worried, please.

SAMUEL: Why the hell not?

SUZIE: Does worry change things into much better things?

SAMUEL: As a rule of thumb—

> to change worry and trouble—impossible
> after one has acquired that engine of proclivity.

> And sometimes, when the weight of the world
> does lie—heavily upon one's shoulders

—Then—something under the surface of things
moves indeed.

But isn't it amazing
how much more comfortable I feel
when I do not look at that woman directly?

SUZIE: That is a fine thing, Samuel. *(She rises)*
But do you mind very much
if I touch you?

SAMUEL: How will you do this?

SUZIE: I will do it—gently, of course.

SAMUEL: Then it should be all right.

SUZIE: Oh, never "all right."

SAMUEL: Why?

SUZIE: Perhaps you don't see it now, Samuel. But look at me.
I am covered in blood.

SAMUEL: What could it be?

SUZIE: My cheeks—

SAMUEL: What?

SUZIE: —covered. My two arms—covered, my thighs, my chest—

ALFREDO: Goddammit.

SAMUEL: Boulevard—mouth—frogs—birds—snout.

SUZIE: I know all about that snout! Just like me. Just like you.
But the blood always shows, Samuel. Do you remember
the famous song titled—

ALFREDO: Don't sing that song.

GABRIELLA *(Approaches with a note)*: La la la la la.

SUZIE: Singing and dancing—in the blood.

ALFREDO: Don't sing that song.

(Suzie reads the note.)

SUZIE: Samuel will have to decide whether he accepts my private invitation.

SAMUEL: If I were able to move my body I would now accept it.

SUZIE: Do you accept it?

SAMUEL: I do not.

SUZIE: Why not?

SAMUEL: Suzie herself, must come to understand—goddammit.

SUZIE: You can't move, Samuel.

SAMUEL: Why such beautiful coquettes cause so much
real pain with the justification perhaps
that coquettes are most painful
when they are most invisible to me?

SUZIE: Does he mean invisible
or does he mean under disguise?

SAMUEL: It's the option— "disguise" to which
I lend most credence.

SUZIE: —In a certain light—
In a certain atmospheric condition
—the coquette-like nature more and more visible— OK
or—even slightly invisible.

(As Samuel is whirled, he is given a sheet.)

And I am now released—am I not?—to say to Samuel
— It is true I am
one possible coquette.
Plus—one possible
being disguised and
therefore able to say this and that, and what I mean is,
this and that
Because of one great
all-encompassing feeling
potentially—inside Samuel himself.

SAMUEL: I have no such confidence.

SUZIE: You see no hints?
—no faint smiles?

(Song: "Mirror, Mirror":)

VOICE:
Mirror, Mirror on the wall
Who's the fairest of them all?

GABRIELLA:
Mirror, Mirror on the wall
Who's the fairest?
Who's the fairest?

SAMUEL: I choose not to look at myself in mirrors, obviously.

SUZIE *(As his blindfold is removed)*: I never smile for you, Samuel.
For involuntary internal reasons.

SAMUEL: Real names
Unnamed
I should think.

SUZIE *(As a stagehand brings her a bouquet)*: Unnamed and yet
unique, of course
So all statement or anticipation
is most certainly erroneous—

SAMUEL: Perhaps the word
"coquette"—shall we use that, though the word itself
is an additional misnomer?

SUZIE: Why not use that name?

GABRIELLA: Gimme.

SAMUEL: My vocabulary—with its serious limitations, of course.

SUZIE: I suggest terms
Other—Than one's vocabulary.

SAMUEL: Such as?—

SUZIE: A forgotten gesture is a possibility—
Widening the potential of the body
—translated into a complex repositioning of limbs.

SAMUEL: My arms and legs—do not easily reconfigure themselves.

SUZIE: Me? Suzie— I can read his deepest thoughts.

(Pause.)

27

SAMUEL: I protest that if you read my thoughts
　　　　you become less beautiful in my eyes
　　　　Because when my own thoughts are inside you
　　　　—my own thoughts—never beautiful
　　　　in and of themselves—
SUZIE: But inside MY body and MY MIND—
　　　　Don't you believe I automatically
　　　　flip-flop?
SAMUEL: You may do that, I suppose.
SUZIE: Did you not think to yourself—this beautiful coquette—
SAMUEL: This is true, of course.
SUZIE *(Rising)*: If this were true
　　　　would I too then be—such a true thing?
SAMUEL: We still know this is true.
SUZIE: Here, Samuel—Here is a powerful drug for us to share.
SAMUEL *(Goes to the drawer and finds it)*: I'd rather not see
　　　　coquettes while I am taking my drugs.
SUZIE: —Coquettes also have taken drugs, Samuel.
SAMUEL: What kind have they taken?
SUZIE: These are the kind
　　　　that leave things as they are.
SAMUEL: But more intense, perhaps.
SUZIE: You will discover
　　　　that leaving things as they are
　　　　is the most intense of possibilities.
VOICE: OK— Not yet.
SAMUEL: I'd still rather not, now, see coquettes.
ALFREDO: Name it!
SUZIE: Do you mean—
　　　　that you would rather not be seen
　　　　by configurations of coquettes
　　　　while you are taking drugs?
SAMUEL: This confuses me.

SUZIE: But coquettes are always
confusing to people.

Which is, of course—
the height of confusion.
The veritable—definition of confusion?
SAMUEL: I claim no special insight— But only
this newly identifiable drug itself—for the hope.
SUZIE: Yes, I never disapprove of drugs.
Does this surprise you?
SAMUEL: Why does this surprise me?
SUZIE: Because there is nothing special
about such intensity, Samuel.
It's like the others.
SAMUEL: Which others?—
SUZIE: Look again, Samuel—
Notice the magic animals.

—Like all animals,
—a little too sure of themselves, which means
—a little bit confused.

(Bears appear.
Pause.)

What do I see? It's the aura which surrounds his
entire physical body—
SAMUEL: Not possible—
Why?
GABRIELLA *(Offstage)*: The sky is falling, Samuel.
SAMUEL: Because if—I had never been born into
this—self-evident world
Is there a way in WHICH—this world

    right now
    would hunger for me at this moment?
SUZIE: I never hunger, Samuel.
ALFREDO AND GABRIELLA: Shy shy shy.
SUZIE: Yes. Here I am.

(Pause.)

SAMUEL: There might be . . . a necessary adjustment in the space
    I now occupy.
GABRIELLA: Don't say that.
SAMUEL: Hard to notice, of course.
GABRIELLA: Don't even think that.
SAMUEL: —But a twist only
       in one possible direction.
SUZIE *(Enters with a panel)*: Wheee!

(Suzie hands off the panel to Alfredo.)

    —And yet—
    sentimental and old-fashioned—and did somebody say
       powerful—
    prostitute—a DEAD prostitute—
    —Such a DEAD fact does or does not erase—
    the one-hundred-percent fact
    of all—always real being existing—
    I see you first!

(Pause.)

SAMUEL: I cannot think the same thing correctly.
SUZIE: Samuel can see that
      we understand more
      than he thinks we understand.

SAMUEL: He never maintains the opposite.
SUZIE: What could be
	the opposite to such a—I see you!

(Pause.)

SAMUEL: My name is Rainer Thompson.
VOICE: Rainer Thompson.
SAMUEL: And I have lost it completely.
SUZIE: You have lost nothing, Samuel.
SAMUEL: My name.
SUZIE: Stop. You have just told me your name, Samuel.
SAMUEL: From this position—

(THUDS.)

	From this position of strength, I am Rainer Thompson
		and I have lost it completely!
SUZIE: The specific characteristic of Rainer Thompson—
	He never lies.
SAMUEL: Right in every way—he avoids expressing himself.
	I certainly do exist. Help me!

(Exits.)

SUZIE: Help me.
	But does Samuel acquire a second name
	in the place of that double name?
SAMUEL: I offer certain familiar letters of the alphabet.
SUZIE: Right. The letter R—
SAMUEL: Yes.
SUZIE: The letter—T.
SAMUEL: Yes.
SUZIE: Shall I look up the name?

SAMUEL: Yes.

SUZIE: Here is a convenient telephone directory with the name—

(Phone rings.)

>Shall I answer?
>Hello?

VOICE: No world.

SUZIE: Here is a man, asking for Rainer Thompson

SAMUEL: Hello? Hello? Hello? Hello?

(Pause.)

>They must have hung up on me.

SUZIE: Oh, the line was disconnected from the beginning, no?

SAMUEL: Or perhaps I too have been lying?

SUZIE: But me—I never never never think you are lying, Rainer Thompson.

SAMUEL: Oh? I never lie.

SUZIE: I have come to know that specific
>characteristic of Rainer Thompson.
>He never lies.

SAMUEL: I never lie.

SUZIE: But one can never know for sure, can one?

SAMUEL: Did the man in the mirror say it first?
>One can never know
>for sure
>—says the same Rainer himself Thompson
>himself, a hero—
>when one says "no one"
>—this indeed becomes "no one"

ALFREDO AND GABRIELLA: Ooo *(Both drop boxes)*

SAMUEL: No matter how many
>interior doors—
>Mr. No One himself—

GABRIELLA: The sky is falling, Samuel.

SAMUEL: Oh, I don't think so.

GABRIELLA: The sky—all by itself.

SUZIE: Possibly—in love, Samuel?

SAMUEL: Oh—I don't think so.

SUZIE: Not even me.

SAMUEL *(Thinks)*: Well—why not, then—
>And through you—the world itself of course.

SUZIE: Ah, how would you prove that?

SAMUEL: Just the opposite, please.

SUZIE: The opposite means—what's opposite.

SAMUEL: Pretend I'm sound asleep.

SUZIE: Not yet true.

SAMUEL: Is my brain doing this to me? Goddammit.

SUZIE: Yes. Let me wake it up with long, out-of date dictionaries.

(Others run through, dropping books.)

SAMUEL: Tried once, failed once.

SUZIE: Yes, I've found a word.

SAMUEL: What word?

SUZIE: Well—
>Emptiness. E—M—P—

SAMUEL: Just what I thought.

*(Exits.
>Reenters.)*

VOICE: Just what I thought.

(Pause.)

SAMUEL: What word?

SUZIE: Just what I thought.

33

(Pause.)

VOICE: Just what I thought.

(Exit.
  Pause.)

End of play
End of play

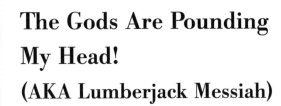

The Gods Are Pounding My Head!
(AKA Lumberjack Messiah)

PRODUCTION HISTORY

The Gods Are Pounding My Head! (AKA Lumberjack Messiah). Produced and presented by the Ontological-Hysteric Theater (Richard Foreman, Founding Artistic Director; Morgan von Prelle Pecelli, Managing Director) at the Ontological at St. Mark's Theater, New York City. January 6–April 17, 2005. Written, directed and designed by Richard Foreman.

DUTCH	Jay Smith
FRENCHY	T. Ryder Smith
BEAUTIFUL GIRL	Charlotta Mohlin

Two lumberjacks, Dutch and Frenchy, enter. A big playground slide is set to one side of the stage, an ancient steam motorcar on the other. A stone tower is at rear that slides from side to side.

DEEP VOICE OVER LOUDSPEAKERS: I won't do it. I won't do it. I won't do it!

(Dutch lifts his axe—and then freezes.)

WHISPERED VOICE OVER LOUDSPEAKERS: "Tendency."

DUTCH: But of course, even a genuine lumberjack knows—when the big heart of the world breaks—then everything breaks.

FRENCHY: You said a mouthful, big Dutch. *(Hands him a hammer)* Go to it.

DEEP VOICE: I am now washing the hammer—WASHING THE HAMMER.

(Demons creep onstage, carrying buckets.)

WHISPERED VOICE: "Tendency."

DUTCH: Even me—lumberjack—I could immediately see what was happening inside my previously—oh-so-beautiful world.

WHISPERED VOICE: "Tendency."

FRENCHY: Excuse me, Dutch—

DUTCH: Totally empty space.

FRENCHY: There's nothing empty around here—not yet.

(Demons run off.)

WHISPERED VOICE: "Tendency."

DUTCH: Why do I feel . . .

FRENCHY *(Throwing down his axe)*: Clunkity-clunk! What you see is what you get.

WHISPERED VOICE: "Tendency."

DEEP VOICE: I'm going to—I'm going to—I'm going to.

DUTCH: I believe what I just heard coming through those big loudspeakers in my brain. Empty space, right?

FRENCHY: Right.

DUTCH: Turning all things of heretofore great depth and profunditoriness—

FRENCHY: Profunda-what, when, where?

DUTCH: Profunda-well—

(He gives a big push to the old-fashioned steam motorcar beside them.)

—into an arena of sissy thin tissue paper—for ladies.

FRENCHY: You.

DUTCH: Me.

FRENCHY: You and me.

DUTCH: Go to it, girly-man.

DEEP VOICE: And I am. And I am. And I am!

FRENCHY *(Climbing to top of playground slide)*: You got me, Dutch.

WHISPERED VOICE: "Tendency."

FRENCHY: You got me! You down and dirty got me. This lonely lumberjack—Frenchy—the immigrant with no papers—

DUTCH: You hear what he calls himself?

FRENCHY: Frenchy is suspended in empty space— Looking for home base earth, I guess.

DUTCH: You are surprisingly close to home, lost, old-fashioned lumberjack.

FRENCHY: That's me, I guess . . .

DUTCH: Here's something else a little old-fashioned: "Come into the garden, Maud—"

DEEP VOICE: Remember when Victorian poet Alfred, Lord Tennyson wrote: "Come into the garden, Maud, for the black bat, night, has flown . . ."

DUTCH:

> Come into the garden, Maud
> I am here at the gate alone
> And the woodbine spices are wafted abroad
> And the musk of the rose is . . .

DEEP VOICE:

> Snug—as a bug in a rug—

FRENCHY *(Sliding down the slide)*: A safe landing for Frenchy—as always.

(Demons return, lifting severed heads out of their buckets.)

That makes me Numéro Uno lumberjack around here.

DUTCH: I'm not going down there—where that Frenchy is—
well, I don't want to talk about it.

DEEP VOICE: This is on a planet that moves around the sun. Not
really. THIS IS ON A PLANET—

DUTCH: Guess what? I've been around the block once—maybe
twice?

WHISPERED VOICE: "Tendency."

DEEP VOICE: MY MENTAL FOAM.

(Demons run off, and the stone tower moves across the stage.)

DUTCH: Good riddance. *(He sees a Beautiful Girl in the door-
way)* What the bejesus? *(She runs off)*

FRENCHY *(At the top of the slide again)*: Hi, Dutch.

DUTCH: Hello, Frenchy.

FRENCHY: Hi, Dutch.

DUTCH *(Speaking to the audience as Frenchy descends)*: Suppose I were to postulate—this is on a planet that moves
around the sun. How would you people deal with that?

*(He starts to exit, stops and turns back to Frenchy who,
startled, bangs against the wall.)*

Don't worry. I'll be back.

FRENCHY *(As Dutch exits)*: If that lumberjack—Dutch—were
to postulate that this is on a planet that moves around the
sun?

WHISPERED VOICE: "Tendency."

*(As Demons enter and one places Ten Commandment Tab-
lets in his arms and Frenchy starts to whirl:)*

FRENCHY: Here I go—One and two and three and four—

BEAUTIFUL GIRL *(Reappearing)*: Stop that crazy round and round business, you lumberjack.

FRENCHY *(Intoning over music)*:
> Thou shalt not fuck other people!
> Thou shalt not use names in vain when they are
>   names of important people!
> Thou shalt bow down to people who are bigger than
>   little people!
> Thou shalt! Thou shalt not!

DEEP VOICE: THE ACTION IS ELSEWHERE.

(A large Byzantine cross dances through at the rear.)

> Going to Istanbul—when I have no ticket to Istanbul!

WHISPERED VOICE: "Tendency."

BEAUTIFUL GIRL *(Sliding down the slide)*: Istanbul!

(The Beautiful Girl dances. Three white objects appear. She hesitantly touches them and screams in pleasure.)

FRENCHY *(Indicating the Girl)*: That's a piece of work there.

DEEP VOICE: Suppose it was the case that you woke up one morning into a world in which the depth and intricacy of your fellow human beings was replaced by a different world in which human beings were—you know—thin, somehow—just surface only—even if that surface seemed clever and quick about the ways of this brand-new, paper-thin world . . .

WHISPERED VOICE: "Tendency."

FRENCHY *(Offering a flask to the Girl)*: Drink it— *(Grabbing it back, drinks)* Drink everything in sight!

WHISPERED VOICE: "Tendency."

FRENCHY *(Going to the white objects)*: I'll look for myself—

(As he reaches out to touch them, the objects scurry off; he turns to Dutch, who has reentered.)

"The world was full of sticks and stones I gathered for a fight—"

DUTCH: "And when a man insulted me I tried to teach him wrong from right."

FRENCHY: Let's find out.

(The Girl climbs to the top of the slide.)

DEEP VOICE: Red door, red door, red door.

WHISPERED VOICE: "Tendency."

FRENCHY *(Blinded by bright light rising)*: Fast Cars!

DUTCH: And really fast women.

BEAUTIFUL GIRL *(From the slide)*: Hey!—
>   There used to be
>   A world of men
>   Who awakened my desire.
>   But now they leave me
>   Cold as ice—
>   They are not kind or deep
>   Or even nice . . .
>   Boo hoo boo hoo
>   I've lost my sheep—What am I to do?
>   Boo hoo!

DUTCH AND FRENCHY *(Singing)*:
>   Little Bo Peep
>   Lost Sheep
>   Deep inside the forest.
>   *(They march together toward the door)*
>   One, two, button my shoe
>   Three, four, out the—

(They are stopped by an invisible wall. Dutch moves the tower out of the way.)

FRENCHY: See? There are some things you do very well, my lumberjack companion. *(Demons enter)* Scoot!

(Frenchy and Dutch run off. The Beautiful Girl puts her feet in buckets and holds two ropes from the ceiling, as the Demons shimmy around her. The two lumberjacks reenter, chopping at the floor with their axes.)

BEAUTIFUL GIRL: See . . . I have dirty feet. *(She sings:)*
 Boo-hoo, Boo-hoo!
 I've lost my sheep
 What am I to do?
 Boo-hoo, Boo-hoo!

WHISPERED VOICE: "Tendency."
DEEP VOICE: Remember, one never enters the future which is immediately behind one. It's a handicap—a real handicap.

(Frenchy plants a big kiss on the Girl's lips. As she wipes off the kiss he comes and winks at the audience.)

You've already seen this before— Therefore it will break your heart.

(Frenchy rubs against the motorcar.)

When you have an emotional attitude towards me, I turn to stone. AN EMOTIONAL ATTITUDE!
BEAUTIFUL GIRL: Big choppitty chop-chop! *(She runs to the top of the slide)*

45

FRENCHY: That's what I do—

DUTCH: They call him—the Little Axe Gesundheit.

FRENCHY: You too.

(The Girl slides down and hits the wall with a thud.)

DEEP VOICE: When you have an emotional attitude towards me, I turn to stone.

(Dutch is given a big vase full of flowers. He doesn't know what to do with it.)

DUTCH: Oh shit. *(He starts to leave, then stops)* Oh shit . . . I forgot something.

(He puts the vase down and crosses to the car. Frenchy starts dogging his footsteps. Dutch whirls around. Frenchy backs up and bangs into the wall.)

Smart move, I guess.

(Dutch goes and cranks the car's engine, and there is a terrible noise.)

FRENCHY AND BEAUTIFUL GIRL *(Over the noise)*: Jesus Christ, cut it out!

(Dutch stops and goes and picks up the flowers, then stops.)

DUTCH: Now this dumb lumberjack forgot something else.

WHISPERED VOICE: "Tendency."

(Dutch hands the flowers to the Girl. Suddenly he holds his chest—)

DUTCH: Jesus!! *(Collapses to the floor)*

FRENCHY *(After a pause)*: Hang in there, Big Dutch.

DUTCH *(Looking up)*: Hey Frenchy—

FRENCHY: Yeah?

DUTCH *(Rising)*: Fuck this life.

FRENCHY: OK.

DUTCH: Suppose I were to postulate—the big engine—

(Again, he holds his heart, then falls with a heavy thud.)

FRENCHY: Hang in there, Big Dutch!!

DUTCH: Double fuck this same life.

WHISPERED VOICE: "Tendency."

(Dutch laboriously rises.)

DUTCH *(Addressing the audience)*: Suppose I were to postulate
the big engine was the heart. How would you people deal
with that?

BEAUTIFUL GIRL: If Mr. Lumberjack—Mr. Dutch—were to postulate the big engine was the heart—I would have to deal
with that.

FRENCHY: Is he dealing with that? Is she dealing with that? Or
am I dealing with that?

BEAUTIFUL GIRL: If Mr. Lumberjack, either Mr. Dutch or Mr.
Frenchy—

FRENCHY: Not me.

BEAUTIFUL GIRL: —were to postulate—

DUTCH *(Sliding in the motorcar, behind the steering wheel)*: Easy
does it, Big Dutch.

BEAUTIFUL GIRL: The big engine was the heart, then I would
have to deal with that.

*(Dutch rocks back and forth in his seat, as a voice intones,
"Jazz, jazz, jazz." Then he reaches under his seat and extracts
a rock.)*

DUTCH: Suppose I were to postulate that this naked—

WHISPERED VOICE: "Tendency."

DUTCH: —and unwashed stone is the heart of the world. Which flies against reason. *(He turns to look back at Frenchy for confirmation)*

FRENCHY: Hi, Dutch.

BEAUTIFUL GIRL *(Irritated, kicking the motorcar)*: If you were to postulate—this stone is the heart of the world that flies against reason, I would have to deal with that!

FRENCHY *(Overlapping)*: —Oh come on, get off it!

DEEP VOICE *(Overlapping, as Demons enter with mirrors and telephones)*: This stone is the heart of the world which flies against reason.

"Immediately, immediately."

Remember: one never enters the future which is immediately behind one.

"The part of him that wanted this was porous."

WHISPERED VOICE: "Tendency."

FRENCHY *(At phone)*: Hello? Is this my long-distance hero? Then how come I'm not getting real information? I'd like some real information.

BEAUTIFUL GIRL *(Sitting in the car)*: I don't belong here in a world where people have speech patterns like idiots. Idiots! Idiots!

FRENCHY: This is not because we displaced lumberjacks are idiots, beautiful girlie. In fact—it's obvious we lumberjacks can speak normal, when the occasion is normal.

BEAUTIFUL GIRL *(Singing)*:
What the hell do I care—Boom. Boom. Boom!

DEEP VOICE: The Action is Elsewhere. Sleep to arrive where the real action is taking place.

(The Beautiful Girl sleeps in the car. A voice far away sings "Oh my Darling, Clementine."

Demons come and peek at the Girl. She awakes with a start and runs out of the car. She hugs the stovepipe which sticks up from its front end.)

DUTCH: What's her problem?

BEAUTIFUL GIRL: Holding on to something solid—and my body starts to shake—

(The Demons poke at her. She screams. She climbs onto the hood of the car.)

BEAUTIFUL GIRL: What's making my body shake?!

DUTCH: What's her problem?

WHISPERED VOICE: "Tendency."

BEAUTIFUL GIRL: Suppose I were to postulate—speeding down the public boulevard in my new polka-dot dress. Can you imagine it?

DUTCH *(Sadly)*: Oh yes, oh yes.

BEAUTIFUL GIRL: —with the imaginary skirt. Yes! Yes! Yes!!— That licks me up and down like fire—my body vibrating like a ferocious engine. Yes! Yes! Yes!

DUTCH: My body too, sometimes. It's going to disappear.

BEAUTIFUL GIRL *(Irritated)*: It's my body we're talking about. It's MY body.

DUTCH *(Sadly)*: Wouldn't you know.

WHISPERED VOICE: "Tendency."

BEAUTIFUL GIRL: I never, never play games—unless?

DUTCH *(Overlapping)*: I know, I know—I know.

DEEP VOICE: WASHING THE HAMMER.

BEAUTIFUL GIRL: But do I catch the eye, suddenly, of a man perhaps—who does call himself "Lumberjack—"

DEEP VOICE: WASHING THE HAMMER.

BEAUTIFUL GIRL: —Messiah?

FRENCHY: Human life—naked and raw—while that multidirectional lady thing—moving not even one tiny feminine muscle.

(The Girl suddenly looks at Dutch, and his eyes burn.)

DUTCH: OW!!

FRENCHY *(As she looks at him)*: OW!

BEAUTIFUL GIRL *(Running to the top of the slide)*: Please— I want my own experience? Name it: "Thick honey, dissolving inside a cup of frozen tea."

DEEP VOICE: What part of him wanted this thing? WHAT PART OF HIM? But just suppose that what this really meant was that the scene of the action was elsewhere, like some atmospheric fluid between people.

(Mirrors are carried to them, and they watch themselves as butterfly nets are also presented.)

BEAUTIFUL GIRL: Peekaboo!

DUTCH: I know—like thick honey.

BEAUTIFUL GIRL: Guess what? I'm going to disappear.

(The butterfly nets go over their heads.)

DEEP VOICE: Bees make honey.

WHISPERED VOICE: "Tendency."

DEEP VOICE: I was always alone, with this redundant tendency to be myself. "TENDENCY."

DUTCH *(Singing)*:
    The busy bumble bee
    Has no time for sorrow
    No time for sorrow.

ALL *(Singing)*:
No time, no time.

DEEP VOICE: Bees make honey.
WHISPERED VOICE: "Tendency."

(Nets come off. They all seize axes.)

DEEP VOICE: Remember when Victorian poet, Alfred, Lord Tennyson wrote—
FRENCHY: The whole world at once.
DUTCH: OK, everybody . . . Suppose I were to postulate—
BEAUTIFUL GIRL: Even me—a girl.
DUTCH: A girl— How would you lumberjack guys—you lumberjack Jacks and Jills . . . How would you deal with that?
WHISPERED VOICE: "Tendency."

(They all chop with axes and hurt their hands and yell in pain. Two giant-sized military medals are passed down the slide.)

DEEP VOICE: Make a machine to be in two places at once.

(Dutch and Frenchy take the medals and hold them up against the wall.)

You've already seen this before, therefore, it will break your heart.
DUTCH: OK, Frenchy— What do we do with these things?
FRENCHY: Well, we hold them—and they get goddamn heavy. And heavier and heavier.

(As music rises, the Demons enter slowly, carrying black globes over their heads.)

51

DEEP VOICE: This is on a planet that moves around the sun: not really.

FRENCHY: How heavy is yours, Dutch?

DUTCH: It's heavy. Maybe mine is even heavier than yours, Frenchy.

FRENCHY *(Coming forward with his medal)*: Hang in there, Dutch. Just hang in there! Hang in there.

(The Demons carrying the globes drift down toward the audience.)

BEAUTIFUL GIRL *(Enters with a tray and a small glass vial)*: Make way lumberjacks, says the reappearing lady with the magic love potion.

FRENCHY: I'd like to, but the results are sometimes contradictory—

DUTCH: This weary, worn-out— I don't know—

FRENCHY: Why don't we name it—the end of our brief, little time in the sun, my friend.

BEAUTIFUL GIRL *(Offering the vial to Dutch)*: Last chance, lumberjack.

DUTCH: OK. I'll think about it.

FRENCHY: Ah, a magic love potion won't save us at this late date. If I deal with such things, we'll both be handling silver darts—

BEAUTIFUL GIRL *(Looking up, her eyes catching the light)*: Oh?

FRENCHY: —from two beautiful eyes, and a powerful fusillade from a delicate pink tongue curled up like a lady's private cannon, including multiple pink private parts.

DUTCH: Not so fast, Woodsman—

FRENCHY: Hang in there, Dutch.

DUTCH: Friend or foe?

FRENCHY: Maybe you're talkin' about yourself, my friend.

WHISPERED VOICE: "Tendency."

DUTCH: Is that possible?

FRENCHY: It's amazing, really—even at this late date, the ladies from—who the hell knows where—still believe he's got, how should I put it— J— A— Z

DUTCH *(Overlapping)*: J? A?

FRENCHY AND DUTCH *(Howling)*: Jazz! JAZZ!

(A tableau of globes and medals.)

DEEP VOICE: A fine fellow. I am now washing the hammer.

(The Girl reenters with a small panel on which a heart is embroidered.)

There was a law requiring all human beings to have a heart embroidered on that piece of clothing covering their chest.

BEAUTIFUL GIRL *(To the audience)*: You are neither my enemy nor the enemies of my enemies— Dutch, Frenchy—lumberjacks! On the other hand— You?

DEEP VOICE: The Lumberjack . . . Messiah.

BEAUTIFUL GIRL: Are you my enemy? *(She runs off)*

DEEP VOICE: Make a machine to be in two places at once.

(Demons run off with their globes, and the Girl reenters.)

BEAUTIFUL GIRL: Taking a dangerous love potion named—guess what? "Fidgit."

DEEP VOICE: "Fidgit." *(The Girl runs off)* The action is elsewhere.

(Dutch is at the side of the stage, still holding his medal. A Demon enters and covers his head with a black hood.)

"Fidgit."

(Frenchy enters, also hooded, led by a Demon who carries a wand that is attached by a rope to the black hood.)

Suppose it was the case that you woke up one morning into a world in which the depth and intricacy of your fellow human beings was replaced by a different world in which human beings were—you know—thin, somehow—just surface only—

(Dutch and Frenchy, still hooded—rock back and forth to dance music.)

FRENCHY: Pancake people—that's us, Dutch—thin and transparent like human pancakes—
BEAUTIFUL GIRL: Pancake people?
FRENCHY: Pancake people! Pancake people!
DEEP VOICE: Two blind mice! Two blind mice!

DUTCH AND FRENCHY *(Singing)*:
    Two blind mice
    See how they run
    Fee fie foe fum.

DEEP VOICE: Remember when Victorian poet Alfred, Lord Tennyson wrote— "MY HERO."
DUTCH: It should be obvious: A lumberjack's work is never done.
FRENCHY: These are the facts, my friends. Chop down everything in the fucking forest so all this new stuff can come crawling through like filthy slimy woodworms.

DUTCH AND FRENCHY *(Singing)*:
    Fee fie foe fum
    See how they run.

DUTCH *(Taking off his hood)*: I can't breathe in this thing.

DEEP VOICE: The Whirlwind! The Whirlwind!

(A big, oversized heart inside a cage is rolled onstage. Thin French baguettes are sticking out of the heart.)

Fidgit! Fidgit! Going to Istanbul—when I have no ticket to Istanbul.

(The Beautiful Girl is now wearing two hearts, plus a piece of raw liver over her face.)

BEAUTIFUL GIRL *(Pointing at the motorcar)*: The big engine goes no place, but the motor is still running.
DUTCH: That's OK, because getting there is half the fun, isn't it?
BEAUTIFUL GIRL: Fun for you maybe, but I'm a human being— and day after day after day— I want good things to eat.
FRENCHY: OK, stuff yourself like a pig—
DEEP VOICE: ISTANBUL!
FRENCHY: And then offer your two hearts to the highest bidder. How about it?
BEAUTIFUL GIRL: Suppose I were to postulate—

(Demons extract the French baguettes from the heart.)

Feed the big engine.

(They stick the baguettes into the car's hood, as if they were sparkplugs.)

DEEP VOICE: Some women had two hearts. *(Dutch holds onto the bread)* The motor is running, the motor is running, the motor is running.
DUTCH: But even a lumberjack knows, when the heart of the world breaks—

55

DEEP VOICE: "Fidgit."

(Dutch holds onto the stovepipe of the motorcar and Frenchy pounds his fist against his own chest.)

You've already seen this before, therefore it will break your heart.

DUTCH: Suppose I were to postulate—

FRENCHY *(Pointing at Dutch)*: He wanted to be—well—fixed: impenetrable like stone.

DUTCH: That's not true.

FRENCHY: Let's find out—

WHISPERED VOICE: "Tendency."

BEAUTIFUL GIRL *(Holding up Ten Commandment Tablets)*: Suppose one of two lumberjacks—

FRENCHY: Me.

DUTCH: No, me.

BEAUTIFUL GIRL: Different from each other like old-timer number one, and old-timer number two—were to postulate: Things fall from the sky. *(She runs to the top of the slide)* This fell from the sky. Hard to believe.

FRENCHY *(As Demons dump items from buckets at their feet)*: It's raining garbage.

DUTCH: What do you know—

FRENCHY: Don't even think about it.

DUTCH: A hammer—

FRENCHY: Two ancient stone tablets.

DEEP VOICE: Things fall from the sky. This fell from the sky.

BEAUTIFUL GIRL: I am now washing the hammer that does not yet belong to me.

(Dutch lifts his axe over his head to chop the heart, and it falls to the floor behind him.)

DUTCH: What happened to my big axe?

FRENCHY: It's behind you, ya dumb lumberjack.

DUTCH: I can't see it—

DEEP VOICE: Don't touch it. Don't touch the big heart. *(Dutch climbs to the top of the slide)*

> Remember, if you disappear by fire—or if you disappear by time—you are making neither of those choices, because it is the world itself which makes such choices on your behalf.

DUTCH: Help me Frenchy— I'm burning up, you gotta help me.

(He lets go and slides to the bottom as Frenchy screams:)

FRENCHY: Don't do it, Dutch!

BEAUTIFUL GIRL *(As Demons lift her high off the ground)*: Suppose I were to postulate—

DEEP VOICE: Snug, as a bug in a rug.

BEAUTIFUL GIRL: Me. Here I am. Things fall from the sky. An object that is impenetrable, like all real objects.

FRENCHY *(Hanging on a rope)*: Suppose I were to postulate—

DEEP VOICE: Snug, as a bug in a rug.

FRENCHY: My body felt better when twisted—how would you guys deal with that?

DEEP VOICE: MY MENTAL FOAM.

FRENCHY: Suppose I were to further postulate—twisting and turning until the lumberjack body was inside out. And in that peculiar and vulnerable condition—

DEEP VOICE: Fidgit!

FRENCHY: —Frozen as it were in the expectation that a beloved mirror image would appear in sunlight so bright—that if I look into such light—that light will blind me. Thank God for that! Thank God! Thank God!

DEEP VOICE: MY MENTAL FOAM!

FRENCHY: The one feeling left in me being the feeling—my insides were on fire.

DUTCH: Just like me. That's Frenchy, but it's just like me.

WHISPERED VOICE: "Tendency."

FRENCHY: Because the beloved for whom I was waitin' in desperation appeared suddenly—like an invisible somebody stepping into that light that blinds all lumberjacks—with my eyes melting into that same fire that burns all other fires. The best fire of all. The real fire. The real fire. The real fire.

DEEP VOICE: MY MENTAL FOAM!

FRENCHY *(Staring at bright light)*: Jesus Christ—my eyes burnin' like two eggs on a hot griddle.

(Dutch and Frenchy scream as their eyes burn, and two fried eggs on a griddle are presented to them.)

DEEP VOICE: The big engine! The big engine was the heart. *(The big, caged heart is lifted into the air)* I am now washing the hammer. *(Dutch and Frenchy grab their axes to attack the heart)* The Heart of the World makes no choices. THE HEART OF THE WORLD!

DUTCH AND FRENCHY *(Singing, given plates of fried eggs)*:
    Look, look, look!
    The big engine was the heart.
    Look, look! Find the hungry heart.
    Look, look! Feed the heart.
    Feed the mind, feed the body of the lumberjack.
    I'm so hungry, deep down hungry!

DEEP VOICE: Bees make honey.

DUTCH AND FRENCHY *(Singing)*:
    Honey for sweetening the eggs.

BEAUTIFUL GIRL *(Singing)*:
Give me the eggs.

DUTCH AND FRENCHY *(Singing)*:
Eggs for the beloved Maud.

FRENCHY *(Singing)*:
But all these eggs for me— Frenchy.

DEEP VOICE: How can I activate my heart?

BEAUTIFUL GIRL *(Singing)*:
Give me the eggs.

(Dutch has moved the stone tower, and discovered behind it a small heart stuck with pins. He brings it forward.)

FRENCHY: See: there are some things you do very well, my lumberjack companion.
DUTCH: What is this?
FRENCHY: A single remaining lumberjack heart.
DUTCH: Right. I'm a useless human being.
FRENCHY: Oh no—
DUTCH: It's true.
FRENCHY: There are some things you do very well.
WHISPERED VOICE: "Tendency."
FRENCHY: Have some eggs.
DUTCH: Oh sure. You get good things in your life, like delicious fried eggs, smothered in honey.
FRENCHY: Oh, you're kidding.
DUTCH: No, no—honey on my eggs. And in two minutes, it's all gone. What's the explanation?

(Demons bring two giant medals to them.)

59

FRENCHY (*Receiving his medal*): Eggs for you, dearie. Because it's apparent that some of us lumberjacks got more important responsibilities.

DEEP VOICE: This redundant tendency.

BEAUTIFUL GIRL: Suppose I was to pin a medal on one of two hungry lumberjacks. How would the other lumberjack deal with that?

(*The mysterious black globes enter at the rear, carried high by Demons.*)

DEEP VOICE: This thing coming.

DUTCH: Guess what? Rough, tough, over the hill—

FRENCHY: Don't say it.

DUTCH: You're right. Because in spite of everything—we still— we still—

(*He sings wistfully:*)

We still have our medals.

FRENCHY: In a world like this, is it still possible for each of us—Dutch—Frenchy—to still be . . . Remember those wonderful fried eggs? I mean—hungry, man.

DUTCH: You're talking about me.

FRENCHY: I'm talking about me.

DEEP VOICE: Being a winner is always, in fact, ludicrous.

DUTCH (*Singing*):
We still have our medals.

DEEP VOICE (*A seven-foot-tall beehive enters slowly*): This thing coming.

FRENCHY: Deep down hungry.

DEEP VOICE: THIS THING COMING! In bad times, the best that can be done is to fail. THE BEST IS TO FAIL!

DUTCH: Wait a minute—that is not what I believe! Even if I believe that—that is not what I believe.

FRENCHY: Suppose I were to postulate, being a winner is, in fact, ludicrous.

WHISPERED VOICE: "Tendency."

DEEP VOICE: Bees make honey.

WHISPERED VOICE: "Tendency."

BEAUTIFUL GIRL: The busy bee has no time for sorrow.

FRENCHY: Well, my little darling— A bee may be landing on ancient, yet immortal, fungi in the middle of the forest.

WHISPERED VOICE: "Tendency."

FRENCHY: Or millions of busy buzzing bees circlin' and circlin' towards a golden, flying saucer in the sky.

DEEP VOICE: I won't do it—I won't do it—I won't do it—!

(As the Voice rises, the three touch the tall beehive, and pull back with a scream, as it burns their hands. They run off-stage.)

BEES MAKE HONEY!

(Demons push the tower across the stage, then point toward the side. Frenchy, Dutch and the Beautiful Girl enter. They stride forward with an eccentric rocking back and forth step to strange music, wearing plumes of white ostrich feathers on their heads, and carrying severed heads that wear crowns.)

FRENCHY *(Slowly pointing toward the horizon)*: "Courage, he said, and pointed towards that land . . ."

DUTCH: Courage! Courage—spoken both as Lumberjack, and one who is here to bring so-called "good news."

FRENCHY: Good news, indeed.

BEAUTIFUL GIRL:
>   The Busy Bee
>   Has no time for sorrow.

FRENCHY: Courage—in the noble voice of the sadly forgotten Victorian poet, Alfred, Lord Tennyson.

(All three step back in shock as giant portraits of Tennyson are quickly hung on the walls.)

DUTCH: The noble Tennyson. Did he not write—

FRENCHY: "Come into the garden, Maud, for the black bat, night—"

DUTCH *(Interrupting him)*: No, no, no. The immortal lines:
>   The Land of Lumberjacks
>   where giant pine trees
>   tumble to the ground
>   The mild-eyed melancholy lotus eaters
>   weep and gather round . . .

FRENCHY: "Courage, he said. Courage—and pointed towards that land." The gods—who fail us once again . . .

BEAUTIFUL GIRL: Guess what— What I like best, is the poem about Maud.

FRENCHY: Those self-same gods—reach out their absent helping hand.

(All three reach their hands forward.)

DEEP VOICE: Remember, remember—if you disappear by fire, or if you disappear by time, you make neither of those choices. Because it's the world itself making such choices on your behalf.

(A giant red bird enters, Demons with feathered headdresses ride on its back. Frenchy, Dutch and Beautiful Girl seize axes and prepare to attack, but suddenly freeze immobilized.)

Handicap, a real handicap.

(Pause, a tableau.)

Suppose it was the case that you woke up one morning into a world in which the depth and intricacy of your fellow human beings was replaced by a different world, in which human beings were—you know—thin, somehow—just surface only— Even if that surface seemed clever and quick about the ways of this brand-new, paper-thin world.

(Demons in feathered headdresses carry in trays bearing many jeweled goblets.)

FRENCHY: Ah, just in time. Multiple servings of a certain . . . magic potion. *(Frenchy, Dutch and Beautiful Girl start drinking from the goblets)* Sometimes—sometimes it works.

(They toss away the empty goblets after drinking, and seize others, as the lights start to fade slowly.)

Sometimes it works . . .

*(They throw away more goblets.
After a while, the lights are completely out.)*

THE END

Idiot Savant

PRODUCTION HISTORY

Idiot Savant. Co-produced by the Ontological-Hysteric Theater (Richard Foreman, Founding Artistic Director; Morgan von Prelle Pecelli, Managing Director) and The Public Theater (Oskar Eustis, Artistic Director; Andrew D. Hamingson, Executive Director). Presented at The Public Theater, New York City. October 27–December 20, 2009. Written, directed and designed by Richard Foreman.

IDIOT SAVANT	Willem Dafoe
MARIE	Alenka Kraigher
OLGA	Elina Löwensohn
SERVANTS	Joel Israel, Eric Magnus, Daniel Allen Nelson

VOICE: Ladies and gentlemen. Ladies and gentlemen. In the course of this evening's performance, the following physical objects will appear on stage: A boxing bag, four golf clubs, a newspaper, two small targets, an oversized golf ball plus snake, a bloody towel, a duck mask, a white spider with spots, a watering can, three boulders wrapped in twine, a yellow suit, two imitation row boats, one tray of fruit, one rolling table, six highball glasses, two white pillows, one large roll of plastic tape, a jeweled wristwatch, one package, gift-wrapped, one jeweled container, plus one blank container, three mirrors with numbers painted on the reverse side, two bows and arrows, one duck in a small cage, one stuffed small mouth plug.

(Idiot Savant, in semi-eighteenth-century dress, with hair piled on top like a Japanese samurai. All women in similar

*dress. Idiot Savant enters with a caged duck, immediately
taken away from him.)*

Let's do that again.

Message to the performers: Do not try to carry this play
forward. Let it slowly creep over the stage with no help,
with no end in view.

MARIE: Oh Idiot Savant—why stuff that provocative den-
tal instrument into your mouth—impeding all possible
"human speech"?

(He takes it out. Pause.)

Thank God, you've removed it.

IDIOT SAVANT: As a result, dear lady—am I no longer capable
of saving us from magic words?

MARIE: But they occur very infrequently.

IDIOT SAVANT: Is it true?

MARIE: Have they begun happening?

IDIOT SAVANT: Are we under attack, Madame?

MARIE: What makes chosen words—magic?

IDIOT SAVANT: Who among us is prepared for an explanation?

MARIE *(Pause, thinks)*: Me?

IDIOT SAVANT: Me?

MARIE: Me!

IDIOT SAVANT *(Pause, then mockingly)*: Me? Me? Me? Me?

MARIE: You produce new levels of confusion—

IDIOT SAVANT: I am interested in confusion, Madame, which
immediately erases the power of OTHER PEOPLE over
my own PRIVATE person—

MARIE *(Thinks)*: Why this word—"me"?

IDIOT SAVANT: Does it evoke—MYSTERIES of the multiple?

MARIE *(Thinks)*: Perhaps with mental adjustments.

IDIOT SAVANT: I sense a GULF rising between us, Madame.

(Pause.)

Am I mistaken in my CHOICE?

MARIE *(She thinks—What choice?)*: I know the Idiot Savant is rarely mistaken.

VOICE: Watch out!

IDIOT SAVANT: Not even this once?

MARIE: Well—*Idiot Savant?*

IDIOT SAVANT: Why "Idiot"?

MARIE: I don't know.

IDIOT SAVANT: Why "Savant"?

MARIE: I still don't know.

IDIOT SAVANT: OK—rarely mistaken—though unnecessary words still pass between us—

MARIE: Must one remember SINGLE words only?

IDIOT SAVANT *(Puts up a hand)*: Be on guard, Madame!

MARIE: Against a WORD?

IDIOT SAVANT: Choose it, please.

MARIE *(Thinks)*: Any word?

IDIOT SAVANT: Why not—

MARIE *(To herself)*: Always "why not"—

IDIOT SAVANT: Make it MAGIC, please?

MARIE: OK.

(Pause.)

Yes!

IDIOT SAVANT: On guard ALWAYS!

(Pause, as she shifts.)

MARIE: I don't know how to be on GUARD against a WORD.

IDIOT SAVANT: Use it.

MARIE: Yes, but—

71

IDIOT SAVANT: On GUARD, always!

Have you decided? Which of two powerful words—holds more MAGIC?

MARIE: Me?

IDIOT SAVANT: Ah!— But is it good for you?

MARIE *(Thinks)*: No.

IDIOT SAVANT: Try word—number two.

(Pause.)

MARIE: Right—

IDIOT SAVANT: Ah?

SERVANTS: Right. Wrong.

MARIE: But why did I say—"right" instead of "yes"? Replacing that more powerful word of proven power—i.e., "yes"?

IDIOT SAVANT: I do not answer. I am an idiot.

(Pause.)

MARIE: I do not answer. I am confused.

(Pause.)

IDIOT SAVANT: But what I PSYCH OUT, Madame—is that your own misplaced "non-talking" and/or gesticulating—DOES *NOTHING* FOR ME, Madame!

VOICE: Watch out.

IDIOT SAVANT: NOTHING!

What was THAT? *(Thinks)* Obviously, delineating a private psychic space—wherein speaking is "off the record"—allowing me to eliminate LESS powerful words—utilizing a roll of HEAVY PLASTIC TAPE.

(He pulls off a piece.)

Which words will this eliminate?

voice: The secret is no longer hidden, friends. Rejoice.

marie: It depends how you use it.

(Pause.)

idiot savant *(Nods)*: It will depend how I use it.

marie: A taped mouth means all POSSIBLE words are eliminated.

idiot savant *(Shrugs)*: Meaning "some" will be eliminated. Try to believe it.

(Pause.
Tapes his mouth.)

marie: A kind of perfection perhaps? The Idiot Savant no longer speaks, making conversation between us very "one-sided." BUT I do understand the best solution might be—to alter one's sense of time passing—

(Clock revealed.)

So that in the past—plus the immediate future—

(She spins once.)

—words spoken by this non-speaking Idiot Savant, occur in some hypothetical—"frozen moment"—

(She hesitates, frowns and reconsiders.
Gets a gift package.)

Here is my "thank-you" gift for the powerful Idiot Savant. But I do wonder if the Idiot Savant will be able to open this gift with a mouth sealed with tape? Because I remember occasions on which his prominent front teeth were used to rip open mysterious packages.

(He removes the tape suddenly; an accompanying noise.)

My goodness— Did that hurt?

IDIOT SAVANT: Your gift so FAR from my physical person, Madame—which I can't possibly open from such a great distance.

MARIE: Then come and take it from me.

(Pause.)

IDIOT SAVANT: Shall I re-tape my mouth?

MARIE: No.

IDIOT SAVANT: I never open a package more than twelve inches from my body.

MARIE *(Thinks)*: Then I put it back into the cabinet.

IDIOT SAVANT: Wait—

VOICE: Too late. Too late.

IDIOT SAVANT: Put it immediately on the table.

MARIE *(Thinks)*: It will be vulnerable to attack.

IDIOT SAVANT *(As Olga enters)*: Attacking a well-intentioned gift? I don't think so.

MARIE: I can imagine a premature opening of my gift.

(Pause.)

IDIOT SAVANT: One must RISK such things.

(She puts the gift onto a table.)

And I shall now seize it myself.

(Olga lunges forward and picks up the gift. Others step back shocked, as she opens it, takes out a watch, and straps it on her wrist. Others aim bow and arrow at his mouthpiece. Pause. All look at the clock, then at the watch.)

VOICE: One, two, three, four, five, six.

OLGA *(Sings)*:
>The creepy man said, "Dear, you need a watch."
>I said, "OK, but don't you . . . Watch me strap it to my body, huh."

MARIE: What MADE THIS HAPPEN! A jeweled wristwatch ruthlessly appropriated— Beneath the gaze of two antique clocks, poised on the shelf behind us.

Three independent agents of time—aiming at THIS ONE MOMENT.

But are such things in fact—out of SYNC? —TOUGH SHIT!

OLGA: The Idiot Savant—who now cannot see—cannot talk— yet does hear all things that tick tock, tick tock and tick tock—

MARIE: Don't stop on my account, please.

OLGA: YOU'RE back, my dear? EVERYTHING stops.

(Pause.)

MARIE: Be ashamed of yourself, my dear.

OLGA: No way.

MARIE: In the presence of this jeweled container which is the representation of the hidden deep mind—trembling in my *very* hands.

(Pause.)

It never opens.

OLGA *(Irritated)*: I know that.

(She gets a second box.)

Know also—a second less decorative container—to better represent that first, jeweled container, which is, in fact, quite VULGAR, dear Marie.

IDIOT SAVANT: A question for both ladies, which neither will answer correctly—pleasing me considerably . . .

VOICE: One, two, three, four, five.

IDIOT SAVANT: Remember this table?

OLGA AND MARIE: Put it down.

OLGA: Immediately.

IDIOT SAVANT: My universal symbol of mental stability, though all such tables can be easily destroyed by a second table.

MARIE: An axe I understand—not a second table—

OLGA: It's obvious, my dear. Tables can be superseded when used for things like—savory dinner choices—because that same activity can move to a second table.

MARIE *(Thinks):* This does not destroy table number one.

OLGA: To supersede something, is always to destroy a first "something else."

MARIE: I shall never—be superseded, bitch.

VOICE: Message to the performers: You have been tricked again.

IDIOT SAVANT: No importance.

I simply reintroduce my justifiably obsessive subject. i.e. "Table—versus . . . *(Thinks and points to head)* — TRIPOD."

MARIE AND OLGA: Why that?

IDIOT SAVANT: Tripod. Which utilizes three legs to rest firmly upon all aberrant surfaces—ending on tip top however— in a single point upon which few earthy "things" can be guaranteed to balance—Obsessive. Got it?

(Pause.)

Yet Mr. Four-Legged Table—vulnerable to the wobble of an uneven floor. Whoopsie, on me!

VOICE: Let's do that again.

IDIOT SAVANT: Whoopsie!

OLGA AND MARIE: Whoopsie daisy.

IDIOT SAVANT: Never mind, because Mr. Four-Legged Table, displays on top a very stable surface upon which THOUGHTS even—may be written down with a lead PENCIL—

MARIE AND OLGA: Oh no.

OLGA: Pointy things.

IDIOT SAVANT: A quandary here—clear thinking, ladies and gentlemen—

VOICE: Ladies and gentlemen, we now assume the considerable responsibility of placing before you the major figures participating in this theatrical event entitled *Idiot Savant*.

IDIOT SAVANT: One, two, three . . . one, two, three . . . one, two three . . . Why is it Mr. Table rather than Mr. Tripod—who does, after all, imitate the characteristics of this same stable, wobbling—IDIOT SAVANT!

(He smashes into a wall.)

MARIE *(Thinks)*: See? My personality is quite stable, in comparison.

(It's nothing of the sort, of course.)

IDIOT SAVANT: And MY personality? Let me think about this with my available instruments—

(He counts on his fingers.)

One—two—three—

OLGA: There is no reason to expect a stable personality inside the *Idiot Savant.*

IDIOT SAVANT: GOOD. Because all numbers that hopscotch through my brain are ODD indeed—going odd one plus two plus three plus four plus five plus six plus seven plus eight plus plus plus.

(He counts on and on.)

MARIE: Wait a minute!— It's every OTHER number that's supposed to be ODD.

OLGA *(Pouring herself a drink)*: Experts are CONFUSED.

IDIOT SAVANT: Experts, these experts are confused, when the Idiot Savant—bounces into empty corners of a potential dining room suddenly filled with amazing brightness. Wow! Wow! Wow! Experts are confused, Madame.

OLGA: Inevitable confusion, inside the mental elevator of an Idiot Savant going back and forth apparently sideways.

IDIOT SAVANT: A code, for such dangerous intensities, Madame.

OLGA: My intensity of choice is up and down—

(She pours and drinks.)

—strong alcohol to dry lips.

(Hugs herself.)

VOICE: The secret is no longer hidden, friends. Rejoice.

OLGA: KISS ME!

IDIOT SAVANT *(Holds up a hand to stop her)*: Lips that shall NEVER taste—demon whisky, Madame!

OLGA: Oh strongest of whiskies— Now! Now! NOW!

IDIOT SAVANT *(Ripping out his gag)*: No other human being moves until I first REACH into this beneficent white light to extract one piece of ripe delicious fruit. Yum yum. How wonderful to imagine nobody in my entire world can experience such things on some permanent basis.

MARIE *(Entering in a row boat)*: Oh powerful Idiot Savant— Notice—I arrive from far away to experience delicious locally grown fruit.

IDIOT SAVANT: A taste only?—

MARIE: What better reason?

IDIOT SAVANT: What I shall offer is fruit in friendship, but never my own private—taste experience, alas.

MARIE: But similar—

IDIOT SAVANT: I know not "similar," Madame— I have no basis for "similar." *(Wipes his lips)*

MARIE: Perhaps I shall row myself back to my point of origin.

IDIOT SAVANT *(Suddenly offers a tray of fruit)*: Delicious fruit?

MARIE *(Stops)*: My brain works against my better judgment.

IDIOT SAVANT: Experts are confused.

MARIE: TAKE back your stupid fruit.

OLGA: Not even a bite?

(She drops the tray and hisses at her, scattering fruit, which Servants gather.)

IDIOT SAVANT: Careful, buddy!

(Exits.)

MARIE: On multiple levels, I protect myself.

OLGA: Experts are confused?

MARIE: Brain first, digestive system, second.

OLGA *(Shrugs)*: Doing research?

MARIE: Not with my stomach?

OLGA *(Considers)*: I prefer brain research, of course.

MARIE: Upside down as usual.

(Cards are pulled off the wall revealing images of fruit on the reverse side. Servants announce their cards one after the other: "Apple, banana, pear, grape, pineapple.")

OLGA *(For each card)*: Expecting no reward, of course.

MARIE *(Thinks)*: Expecting no happiness.

OLGA: Expecting no emotional cornucopia raining down upon EITHER of us.

(Enter Idiot Savant, in a glass bubble row boat.)

OLGA: But from across which vast ocean of non-utilizable desire comes this hallucination, ensconced in that nautical thing to catch my attention—and to protect himself from possible germs, probably.

IDIOT SAVANT *(Into built-in megaphone—over loudspeaker)*: You dislike me very much, Madame.

OLGA *(Thinks)*: Is it me—?

MARIE: It's me first, my dear.

IDIOT SAVANT: Never speak about such matters of the heart, unless accompanied by heartrending appeals from ladies such as yourselves—

MARIE *(To Olga)*: You first, dear—

OLGA: I think not, dear.

IDIOT SAVANT: Dear lady of choice—

Stimulate me further by dressing in my provided yellow suit.

(A yellow suit has appeared.)

OLGA: Is this a proposal?

IDIOT SAVANT: —Which will powerfully protect us from our shared problem of potentially mutual desire.

OLGA: I need no protection.

IDIOT SAVANT: Is it not best to protect ourselves from human beings dangerously attracted to hundreds of other human beings?

(Pause.)

OLGA: I alternatively propose that this cutie pie Idiot dresses in his own yellow suit—within which he was hoping perhaps, I would TOTALLY become invisible.

IDIOT SAVANT: This shall become my buffer against unavoidable reality—MEANING, of course . . . private desire now magnetized. MEANING all OBJECTS of my desire—RUSHING toward me with overwhelming speed—

(He and Olga spin and sing "Yessss!" then stagger to a stop.)

Such speed— Leaving desire far behind such—self-same desire.

OLGA: Which is why we adore—always desirable Idiot Savant— above all other Idiot Savants.

(Loud knocking starts.)

IDIOT SAVANT: My God— What KNOCKS loud enough to put me permanently to sleep?

OLGA *(Thinks)*: Knocking should never put people to sleep.

IDIOT SAVANT: In my yellow suit—I am able to answer the apparent paradox— A faraway locked door, in some "other" room, where two physical ears no longer wide awake.

OLGA: Knock, knock, knooooooooooock!

IDIOT SAVANT: But replace those raw vocal knuckles, Madame, banging against my private doors and windows—

OLGA: Knock knock knock . . .

MARIE: Knock! Knooooock!

OLGA: Knock.

(Pause.)

IDIOT SAVANT: Experts are confused, of course—
      which neither frightens nor disorients an Idiot Savant,
      having recently discovered himself trapped inside
      the city of his bad, bad dreams—where—
      one elderly gentleman reaching towards his
      two vulnerable shoulders
      Where snow white wings are trying to SPROUT,
      —an optical illusion of course—
      This elderly gentleman, with hair—
      now all white—
      —from the heights of his
      considerable contempt exclaiming—
      "If wings are to be imagined, young man—
      they had best not bust my balls—
OLD MEN: Come on down, down, down, sonny boy!
IDIOT SAVANT: —trying to fly!"

(Two white-haired old men have entered carrying boulders.
They set them down around the floor.)

      OK—
      Does he lose his balance?
      Does he fall towards the end of his drop-dead life—
      approaching rapidly—since everything done till now—
      Help me, help me.
MARIE: No help here.
IDIOT SAVANT:
      All sufficiently fine
      To touch all four corners of his oh-so touchable soul,
      endured "just long enough"
      to endure this "being touched"?

MARIE: Oh no.

OLGA: Oh no.

IDIOT SAVANT: Just what the doctor ordered
    except
    nobody remembers the NAME of this mysterious
        doctor—
    — Looking into a real mirror
    except—
    nothing inside that mirror— Get it?
    So why did "guess-who" wait to be so old
    before he finally GOT IT!
    And oh—believe me
    now he DOES NOW GET IT!
    I hope-a-hope-a-hope-a-hope—

MARIE: Why call him Idiot Savant, when he falls over things so long anticipated?

IDIOT SAVANT: Because, my dear—he does change costumes many times in preparation for what should be obvious—

VOICE: And this Idiot Savant, inside degrees of "being disguised"
    Though recognizable—
    Inside that same excellence of disguise.

IDIOT SAVANT: But this face of mine, in fact— REAL?
    Or simply a "THING" that whispers
    To myself at CRUCIAL moments—

MARIE: My God. Remember the girl in the rowboat turning upside down? That was me.

IDIOT SAVANT:
    Reconnect with
    all things.

MARIE: Me.

IDIOT SAVANT: Always—

MARIE: Doll-like me under the midnight moon—

IDIOT SAVANT: My own "preeminence"—

voice: One, two, three, four, five.

idiot savant: Staring at the moon over my head where pale moon boulders "are spelling out the real name of this second heavenly body—"

(He drops his boulder, thinks—frozen.)

A potent hint— Is something wrong?

(He is given another boulder.)

When my own two hands no longer obey my mental commands, but act of their own free will?

olga: That can't be proven.

idiot savant: But I'm never wrong. *(Drops his boulder)*
Oh shit!
I shall order my two hands to move to my Idiot face.

olga: Accomplished with finesse.

idiot savant: I now order my two hands—move to my Idiot face. Come on. Come on.

(Nothing happens, he shrugs.)

olga: I hope this is nonsense?

(Another boulder given, and dropped.)

marie *(Orders him)*: Try moving them without saying "hands move."

(Then—they move differently.)

idiot savant *(Thinks)*: Why do I solve mysteries, when other people cannot solve such mysteries?

(Pause.)

OLGA: Experts are confused.

MARIE: If solving a mystery is never possible—then don't call that a mystery.

IDIOT SAVANT *(Cries out)*: Please help!

(Pause.)

MARIE: Sweet Marie gives no help.

IDIOT SAVANT: Me neither. No help.

OLGA: Ladies and gentlemen: The Idiot Savant. The great Idiot Savant. Yes, he's talking. He's walking. He's still talking.

IDIOT SAVANT: I'll be back. I'll be back. I'll be back.

(Exits.)

MARIE: He disappears?

OLGA: You're at fault, my dear.

MARIE *(Thinks)*: HE has the right to disappear? Whenever he chooses?

OLGA *(Confirming)*: Making it unpleasant obviously for both of us.

MARIE: Oh, yes— Idiot Savant ONCE— Idiot Savant TWICE—

OLGA: Which Idiot Savant are we talking about?

MARIE: Himself in person.

This entire play from beginning—to end.

OLGA: Which could be a most unpleasant memory of course. Two of us invisible without the desire to be invisible.

(Both move behind freestanding screens, and peep out of face holes cut out of painted spider bodies.)

MARIE: When I turn invisible, it's never apparent—apparently.

OLGA *(Sings, with chords played)*:
>Marie Miss Muffet
>On her very tough
>Tough Tuffet
>Bottom down first
>Here comes the worst—

(Crowns offered them, as a big framed spider descends and hangs over them.)

MARIE: Now I remember myself—Idiot Savant inside this play titled *Idiot Savant*—Thank God without filling completely this entire stage.

OLGA: The Idiot Savant fills this whole play—this is very apparent.

MARIE: Not quite.

OLGA *(Thinks, sings)*:
>Down comes lady spider
>Sitting down
>Beside her

MARIE: Insolent fool.

OLGA: Never call me a fool, my dear—though, yes yes yes, I may be both insolent and foolish—wishing never to be characterized as whatever it may be that I may indeed be. Yes yes yes.

MARIE: Me too, my dear. I am full of equally strong feelings— and it follows that when I observe myself, I observe also— my superior well-spread table—

(She rips open her blouse and thrusts out her chest.)

OLGA: Are you going nuts?

MARIE: Confirming my right to characterize however I choose, all others with table not equally "well-spread."

OLGA *(Frowns, ripping open blouse)*: Insolent fool.

MARIE: Are you nuts?

OLGA *(Suddenly worried)*: Why not? When a giant spider is grabbing me by the nose!

(Suddenly scared, they cover themselves and scream.)

VOICE: Rejoice.

(Thunder.)

The secret is no longer hidden, friends. Rejoice.

OLGA: Yes. We are both going nuts.

(Suddenly a backdrop slides onstage, with roses and bees and ducks. The spider still dangles.)

MARIE *(Startled)*: We are nuts to begin with apparently—because of bizarre spiritual factors filling nooks and crannies of a bizarre theatrical performance—

(Idiot Savant enters, watering flowers. Servants aim bow and arrow at him.)

IDIOT SAVANT: Ooh, I'm back.

MARIE: But if HE too goes nuts too, then there is no objective criteria against which to MEASURE the going nuts of you, me, or anybody else I can think of.

MARIE: I believe this play by the name of *Idiot Savant*—hopes to become wiser than individual characters contained within its pages.

IDIOT SAVANT: Having captured this dangerous intruder— now I reveal an even more unsettling reality. To be precise— Before being this character inside this play *Idiot Savant*—I was once this same character—trapped inside an even more disturbing play entitled—*Arrogant Fool.* Arrogant fool.

MARIE: I don't like imagining that play.

OLGA: I will never imagine that play.

IDIOT SAVANT: Bring to mind now, a second forgotten play titled— *Magic Words.* That was already me! THAT WAS ME!

MARIE AND OLGA: *(Singing):*
    Try to remember—

OLGA *(Stops):* But I remember nothing—

VOICE: The secret is no longer hidden, friends. Rejoice. Rejoice.

IDIOT SAVANT: The Beginning: *(Finger up)* The Middle—*(Second finger up)*

(Servants bring flowers; Idiot Savant is baffled. Olga reappears through curtain and poses with her hands on her hips. Idiot Savant gives her flowers. Pause. Thunder.)

The end of my reign approaches, ladies. After which I shall come to know even more frightening experiences.

OLGA *(Angry):* My experience charts itself on a grid—which is no longer my real experience.

IDIOT SAVANT: OK. Maybe this is forever.

(He runs off through the curtain.)

VOICE: WATCH OUT! WATCH OUT!

MARIE: There is no person—behind his person.

VOICE: WATCH OUT!

(Idiot Savant appears through the curtain with a duck mask.)

OLGA *(Into screen)*: How many versions of him do exist however?

IDIOT SAVANT *(Lowering his mask)*: HUNDREDS, plus— A hundred, plus— A hundred. Plus one.

(He runs to give the mask to Olga, and she puts it on her face.)

"Foolish wo-man"

VOICE: Watch out!

IDIOT SAVANT *(Runs to Marie)*: "Foolish wo-man"

MARIE: Even when I find you remarkable— That does hurt—

IDIOT SAVANT: She's been caught!

MARIE: Stay away from me.

IDIOT SAVANT: Your attention is caught, my dear—meaning— that I am the one most DEEPLY caught. Being SMOTHERED, my dear—by such SMOTHERING attention—

MARIE *(To the audience)*: OK. Loving or not loving. Why bother?

(She dashes upstage, stops and whirls to face the audience.)

Bye-bye FOREVER! *(Muttering)* Arrogant bastard.

(Exits.)

IDIOT SAVANT: Thank you for leaving—

VOICE: You have been tricked again, my friend.

IDIOT SAVANT: Oh, I don't think so.

(The red curtain opens—Olga is there, a deep room, a chandelier. She fans herself, agitated.
Harpsichord music.)

OLGA: To you too!

Coming to understand this play, named *Idiot Savant*, says all by itself "I will always exist for myself!"

But!—If the play *Idiot Savant* says such words, does it then become one more Idiot character?

IDIOT SAVANT: Look no further, Madame, because I am always myself inside the *Idiot Savant*! Though I am still the . . .

MARIE *(Reenters)*: Allow me to reenter this long-lost play.

IDIOT SAVANT: But it was never lost.

MARIE *(Thinks)*: But apparently it's been found because otherwise, would I be able to "re"-enter it? I do not think so.

IDIOT SAVANT: Must I say "yes"?

MARIE: No!

IDIOT SAVANT *(Thinks)*: OK. First, I say "no" and I capture you inside this *Idiot Savant*, Madame.

MARIE: If I am totally inside the *Idiot Savant*— What I should be hearing is this play, this play itself—doing "its very own speaking" instead of the *Idiot Savant*.

VOICE: WATCH OUT!

(Pause. Big Duck enters rear. All see it, then pause. Then continue.)

IDIOT SAVANT: But when I stop speaking—there is silence. And I no longer hear the play *Idiot Savant* speaking.

(Pause.)

IDIOT SAVANT *(Quietly)*: Is nobody speaking?

(Pause.)

OLGA: Is it because there are no real human beings?

IDIOT SAVANT: Which is of no real importance in the great scheme of things.

MARIE: Flesh-and-blood human beings hear speaking, when there is speaking.

(All whirl and see Big Duck. Though they have already seen it. Perplexed. They turn back, compose themselves.)

Look what came into this room!

IDIOT SAVANT: OK. Speaking now, with REAL WORDS to drive REAL PEOPLE to REAL PREDICTABLE DISTRAC-TION!?

(Smashes against a wall.)

Ow! "What do I see? What do I think I see?!"

MARIE *(Exploding)*: One day I too shall come to understand idiotic ideas pass through my head like flashes of lightning—

(Flash and crash.)

IDIOT SAVANT *(Ecstatic—sings)*:
    Look at me now, everybody, with two little wings!
    Quack! Quack! Quack! Look, Ma, no hands!

(He waddles from the room, quacking in Duck idiocy. More thunder and lightning.)

MARIE: My current problem is as follows:
    The Idiot Savant, and the mystery of his irrational behavior remain the most interesting subject I can think to talk about.
    But since he apparently doesn't exist . . .
OLGA: I think—she thinks he exists.

(Thunder and lightning. They scream as lights go out.)

VOICE: Back to the beginning.

MARIE: If he—or it—or something equivalent does not certifiably exist.

OLGA: This is not for public discussion.

(Pause.)

MARIE: I say things openly.

OLGA: "Foolish woman!"

MARIE: I understand why you are frightened.

OLGA: Me? Frightened? Ha.

(Pause.)

MARIE: Powerful creatures could be spying on us.

(Pause.)

OLGA: It's POSSIBLE that "you-know-who" is watching us through . . . How do you say . . . peepholes.

VOICE: Watch out.

MARIE: A Godlike Idiot wastes his time—"peeking" at YOU AND ME?

OLGA: Now you call him a God?

MARIE: I do not imagine him PEEKING.

(Pause.)

OLGA: Well I NEVER imagine him peeking.

VOICE: Watch out! Watch out!

(Curtain closes.)

MARIE: Obviously, he has many disguises.

OLGA: Obviously.

MARIE *(Irritated)*: A wild beast—

VOICE: Let's do that again.

MARIE: Howling at midnight.

OLGA: You're changing the subject, bitch.

MARIE *(Holds her head between her fingers)*: OK. A lily-white swan in the wild bulrushes getting fucked. Fucked. Fucked! Fucked! Fucked! Fucked! Fucked! Fucked!

OLGA *(Overlapping)*: My God— See what's happening here?

MARIE *(Pause, looks back)*: A giant duck.

(Pause.)

OLGA: That's very stupid.

MARIE: A psychotic Giant Duck. Chew on that, dear Olga.

OLGA: I will never allow myself to bite into the flesh of a god himself. And I really mean that. Duck plus god equals stupid.

(Curtain opens.)

(Sees Big Duck led by Idiot Savant) NO! That giant duck is no longer allowed in this room— Never. Get out. Get away. Never come back. Don't come in here. Don't even think about it.

VOICE: Watch out!

MARIE: Careful, my dear—offend this Giant Duck, who possibly returns just after midnight to slice us to pieces—

OLGA: Even in jest, don't say things like that.

MARIE: Fear surfaces in somebody I happen to know quite well.

(Pause.)

OLGA: I don't like thinking about it!

MARIE *(Sings)*:
"Naked fear"

(Stops singing) Get up off the floor, bitch.

OLGA: I fell down on my nose! Help me, help me—

IDIOT SAVANT: Ow! Me too—

(He rubs his nose.)

My nose! My nose—

OLGA: What I hurt was my nose when I fell down.

IDIOT SAVANT: Me too, apparently!

MARIE: Double noses need fixing—

OLGA: Stop talking about my nose, bitch!

DEEP VOICE: NOSE.

IDIOT SAVANT: My nose.

OLGA *(Pause, looks around)*: Whose nose is being publicly discussed?

IDIOT SAVANT *(Rubbing his nose again)*: Her nose?— My nose?

VOICE: NOSE.

(Pause.)

IDIOT SAVANT: If a giant duckbill nose does perhaps EXCITE my imagination—

VOICE: NOSE.

IDIOT SAVANT: Activating "unclassifiable emotions"?

OLGA: I will not think about this—

DEEP VOICE: NOSE!

IDIOT SAVANT: No longer shall I deny myself a spectrum of very peculiar feelings—

DEEP VOICE: NOSE! NOSE! NOSE!

(Pause.)

IDIOT SAVANT *(Overlapping)*: Nose nose nose.

I shall no longer deny this quivering inside one agitated Idiot Savant— Confessing to all present, that this is—too much! Much too much!

(He crashes into a wall and staggers back, spinning to the sound of a duck honk.)

—Duck psychic depth—

VOICE: Obviously.

IDIOT SAVANT: Duck, ducky! Duck!

—This singular Duck I do know inside myself—

MARIE: Smashing into walls could be a contributing factor— No!

IDIOT SAVANT: If this Great Duck, surprising us all, now chooses to enter the dining room of one always hungry—human Idiot Savant—

OLGA: Me too, but hungry for life, both raw and perfect.

IDIOT SAVANT: Yes—this Great Duck as my guest—had nevertheless, remember! Duck in the first instance—

VOICE: Obviously. Obviously.

IDIOT SAVANT: Meaning—"DUCK EDIBLE." As in—DUCK— Have some delicious Duck—

DEEP VOICE: I would prefer, I would prefer roast beef sandwiches.

IDIOT SAVANT: My God, is a Duck talking?

VOICE: I would prefer—A roast beef sandwich.

IDIOT SAVANT: One minute, please! Before Duck eats—roast beef—or spaghetti—or cream cheese on toast— Duck is ordered to fulfill first the destiny of all specifically conscious human beings—and therefore—necessarily first— SELF EAT RIGHT?

VOICE: The secret. The secret.

OLGA: This is not my necessity.

IDIOT SAVANT: This is so self-evident, my dear—

OLGA: No creature EATS ITSELF—

DEEP VOICE: Normal life.

IDIOT SAVANT: See what I was saying?

DEEP VOICE: Normal life.

IDIOT SAVANT: The truth. Always the truth.

DEEP VOICE: Sitting in my easy chair.

MARIE: What chair?

IDIOT SAVANT: This is normal?

DEEP VOICE: Reading my evening newspaper—

(Offered a newspaper, Idiot Savant grabs it away.)

IDIOT SAVANT *(Opening it)*: Oh, this is so normal—

DEEP VOICE: Smoking tobacco in my favorite pipe clenched between big duck lips—

OLGA: Duck fat lips. Guess what very disturbing picture flashes into my mind—

IDIOT SAVANT: Don't say it!

OLGA: When a giant duckbill sticks out from the middle of a duck face . . .

VOICE: Watch out!

OLGA: Which can hardly be called a face—

DEEP VOICE: Insulting a Duck. Well done, well done.

IDIOT SAVANT: I do apologize to my Duck friend—

MARIE AND OLGA: Duckbill. Duck Bill.

IDIOT SAVANT: For the continual rudeness of my fellow beings—

OLGA: I don't insult ducks on purpose.

IDIOT SAVANT: We make immediate amends, however—by inviting this Duck to join us in a friendly game—of interspecies golf.

MARIE AND OLGA: Golf ball. Golf ball.

DEEP VOICE: What human beings name as the grotesque in life—

MARIE AND OLGA *(Singing, linking arms)*:
> Duck Bill! Duck bill!

IDIOT SAVANT: Beauty hides in strange places, ladies!

OLGA: Wait a minute. Try hitting this available golf ball.

IDIOT SAVANT: Me? Me? Me? Me?

MARIE: I dropped my golf bag.

IDIOT SAVANT: Or this duck?

OLGA: Isn't it OBVIOUS? A big duckbill nose will interfere with this duck's ability to play a normal game of normal golf.

MARIE: Duck missed big, I think.

IDIOT SAVANT: Not quite—Not quite.

OLGA: Missed again.

MARIE: Why not admit it?

IDIOT SAVANT: Golf ball missed— Yes, unfortunately.

MARIE AND OLGA *(Singing)*:
> Duck bill, duck bill—

IDIOT SAVANT: Nevertheless, nevertheless cruel lady humans— "BULL'S EYE" indeed.

VOICE: You have been tricked again. Back to the beginning.

IDIOT SAVANT: Being herein demonstrated to otherwise unfortunate
> HUMAN BEINGS—One tiny factor, making it more satisfactory perhaps, to be a human THING—rather than to be a DUCK THING! Watch this everybody.

VOICE: Ladies and gentlemen, message to the performers. Rejoice.

IDIOT SAVANT: OK. I correct myself slightly—Since human never translates into "TOTAL" SATISFACTION— Only a bit MORE SATISFACTION in comparison.

OLGA AND MARIE: Oh no.

IDIOT SAVANT: In comparison to "what"?

DEEP VOICE: Arrogant bastard people.

IDIOT SAVANT: This is unbelievable. Standing before you, my duck friend—is no arrogant bastard. I can prove this immediately.

DEEP VOICE: Goodbye forever.

(Big Duck exits.)

IDIOT SAVANT: Forever?

VOICE: Watch out!

IDIOT SAVANT: Now I scrape clean this total piece of—but why bother?

This almost nothing, habitually called—called—
Ah-ah-ah-ah-ah!

OLGA: Forget about meaningless NOISES, please? And decide to give things one-hundred-and-one new and exciting names.

IDIOT SAVANT: And YOU will choose them. Oh I don't think so— *(Turns to Marie and orders)* But YOU will choose them—!

MARIE: First I will choose to say—
Ah-ah-ah-ah-ah!

OLGA: NOTHING!

IDIOT SAVANT: Who heard what I heard?

OLGA *(As she pours herself a drink)*: My carefully considered conclusion is as follows: All Idiot things turn powerful the minute the Idiot Savant says this is what happens.

(She raises glass, then drinks.)

IDIOT SAVANT: No panic, ladies.

MARIE: No visible panic in ME, at least.

VOICE: Rejoice.

IDIOT SAVANT: Great Duck, come back. Get back in here, big duck, you know who I mean.

VOICE: Arrogant bastard people. Goodbye forever.

IDIOT SAVANT: Oh shit I forgot.

MARIE: Don't do that.

IDIOT SAVANT: It never comes back.

MARIE: "Duck language."

OLGA: I have heard this. I do not choose to believe this.

MARIE: These are facts far beyond facts, my dear.

OLGA: Quack quack quack. I can do this easily.

MARIE: My memory of such secret languages with my eyes shut tight.

OLGA: Then my congratulations.

MARIE: Great Duck, I appeal to you since no one else ever helps me.

VOICE: No help thank you.

OLGA: Oh.

IDIOT SAVANT: Shut up when there's more screaming to come.

MARIE: If I say— Please?!—

VOICE: Too late. Much too late—

MARIE: Understand unfortunate reality— Up till now I was TOTALLY SHY about asking a duck to help a human being.

DEEP VOICE: SHY with me?

MARIE: Oh shit.

DEEP VOICE: Rejoice. Rejoice.

MARIE: Oh shit. Oh shit. Oh shit.

IDIOT SAVANT: Shit. Shit. Silence.

> All things are yet thinkable inside a powerful mind,
> which does express itself eventually in apparent babble,
> non-translatable into known languages,
> thank goodness for that— OK?
> Guess what. Running up as usual against—"MAGIC WORDS"

Words that do—smash—this small mental, mental,
   mental mechanism into TINY pieces—

VOICE: Rejoice.

IDIOT SAVANT: Preparing to ROLL over the cold unfriendly floor
   in CALCULATABLE frenzy—just wait—
      —All words chosen—to express REAL THINGS inside
      This—Idiot Savant— Nothing!
      This—full—of nothing—
      SO VERY VERY—
      —full full full full full full—!

DEEP VOICE: No namable knowledge here, perhaps?

VOICE: Watch out!

DEEP VOICE: But—take it as it comes, my friends.
   Just do that much, and immediately—
   Discovering in fact— You do GET IT after all, my
      friends.
   You really "get it" in the end. And that's a fact.

IDIOT SAVANT: Now, wait a minute. I forgot something important.

VOICE: Ladies and gentlemen. Because the play is suddenly
   over, the actors have all gone elsewhere. And now you
   too, ladies and gentlemen, must now go elsewhere. The
   play being over, the stage being empty, and the exit doors
   being opened to invite you into a future very much like
   the past. Indeed, very much like the past. Which is all you
   need to know, ladies and gentlemen, all you need to know.

THE END

RICHARD FOREMAN is the founder and artistic director of the not-for-profit Ontological-Hysteric Theater in New York City (founded 1968). Foreman has written, directed and designed more than fifty of his own plays, both in New York City and abroad. He has received numerous awards and citations, including OBIE awards for Directing, Best Play, and Sustained Achievement; an Annual Literature Award from the American Academy of Arts and Letters; a Lifetime Achievement in the Theater Award from the National Endowment for the Arts; the PEN/Laura Pels Foundation Master American Dramatist Award; a MacArthur "Genius" Fellowship; the Edwin Booth Award for Theatrical Achievement; a Ford Foundation play development grant; a Rockefeller Foundation playwrights grant and a Guggenheim Fellowship for Playwriting. In 2004, he was elected Officer of the Order of Arts and Letters of France. Since the early 1970s, his work and company have been funded by the NEA and NYSCA, in addition to many other foundations and private individuals.

His archives and work materials were acquired by the Bobst Library at NYU in 2004.

The Ontological-Hysteric Theater was located in the historic St. Mark's Church-in-the-Bowery, in New York City's East Village neighborhood from 1992 to 2010, and served as a home to Foreman's annual productions as well as to other local and international artists. During these years Ontological began presenting emerging theater artists. The program, to be known together with the theater as the Incubator Arts Project, continued to produce and present at St. Mark's Church from 2010 until it closed in 2014, led by director-producers Shannon Sindelar and Samara Naeymi, designer Peter Ksander, production manager Brendan Regimbal, and composer Travis Just.

In the early 1980s a branch of the Ontological-Hysteric Theater was established in Paris, funded by the French government.

Foreman's plays have been co-produced by such organizations as New York's Public Theater/New York Shakespeare Festival, La MaMa, The Wooster Group, the Festival d'automne in Paris and the Vienna Festival. He has collaborated (as librettist and stage director) with composer Stanley Silverman on eight music-theater pieces produced by the Music-Theater Group and the New York City Opera. He wrote and directed the opera *What to Wear* (music by Michael Gordon), which was produced in 2006 at CalArts's REDCAT Theatre in Los Angeles. He has also directed and designed many productions with major theaters around the world, including *The Threepenny Opera*, *The Golem* and plays by Václav Havel, Botho Strauss and Suzan-Lori Parks for The Public Theater/New York Shakespeare Festival; *Die Fledermaus* for the Paris Opera; *Don Giovanni* for the Opera de Lille; Philip Glass's *Fall of the House of Usher* for American Repertory Theatre and the Maggio Musicale in Florence; *Woyzeck* at Hartford Stage; *Don Juan* at the Guthrie Theater and The Public Theater/New York Shakespeare Festival; Kathy Acker's *The Birth of the Poet* at the Brooklyn Academy of Music and the RO Theater in Rotterdam; and Gertrude Stein's *Doctor Faustus Lights the Lights* at the Autumn festivals in Berlin and Paris.

He wrote and directed his first feature film, *Strong Medicine*, in 1983. His second feature film, *Once Every Day*, came out in 2012 and was featured in both the New York Film Festival and in the Berlin Film Festival. It is distributed by Re: Voir Video. His more recent films, *Now You See It Now You Don't* (2017) and *Mad Love* (2018) are available for viewing at PennSound Cinema.

He holds degrees from Brown University (BA, Magna Cum Laude, Phi Beta Kappa) 1959; Yale School of Drama (MFA, Playwriting) 1962; and an Honorary Doctorate from Brown University, 1993. He was born in New York City on June 10, 1937.

There are numerous collections of Foreman's plays, and books that study his work. Works by Foreman include: *Plays with Films* (Contra Mundum Press, 2013); *Bad Boy Nietzsche! and Other Plays* (TCG, 2007); *Paradise Hotel and Other Plays* (The Overlook Press, 2001); *No-Body: A Novel in Parts* (The Overlook Press, 1996); *My Head Was a Sledgehammer: Six Plays* (The Overlook Press, 1995); *Unbalancing Acts: Foundations for a Theater* (Pantheon Books, 1992; TCG, 1994); *Love & Science: Selected Music-Theatre Texts* (TCG, 1991); *Reverberation Machines: The Later Plays and Essays* (Station Hill Press, 1985); and *Richard Foreman: Plays and Manifestos* (New York University Press, 1976).

Books that devote their entirety or a chapter to Richard Foreman and his work include: *Richard Foreman: an American (partly) in Paris* by Neal Swettenham with Richard Foreman (Routledge, Taylor & Francis Group, 2018); *ABCDery of Richard Foreman*, Anne Berevolitch (Editions du Sud, Paris, 1999); *Die Bühne als Szene Denkens*, Markus Wessendorf (Alexander Verlag, Berlin, 1998); *Directors in Rehearsal: A Hidden World*, Susan Letzler Cole (Routledge, 1992*)*; *The Director's Voice: Twenty-One Interviews*, Arthur Bartow (TCG, 1988); *In Their Own Words: Contemporary American Playwrights*, David Savran (TCG, 1988*)*; *The Other American Drama*, Marc Robinson (The Johns Hopkins University

Press, 1994); *Postmodernism and Performance*, Nick Kaye (Macmillan, 1994); Richard Foreman, edited by Gerald Rabkin (PAF Books: Art + Performance/The Johns Hopkins University Press, 1999); *Richard Foreman and the Ontological-Hysteric Theater*, Kate Davy (UMI Research Press, 1981); *Theater at the Margins: Texts for a Post-Structured Stage*, Erik MacDonald (University of Michigan Press, 1993); and *Tradizione e Ricerca*, Franco Quadri (Giulio Einaudi, Editore, 1982).